ESSENTIAL
pantry
COOKBOOK

ESSENTIAL
pantry
COOKBOOK

80 Easy Recipes and 100 Creative Variations to Make the Most of On-Hand Staples

JEN CHAPIN

Photography by Darren Muir

ROCKRIDGE
PRESS

Interior and Cover Designer: Patricia Fabricant
Art Producer: Samantha Ulban
Editor: Cecily McAndrews
Production Editor: Ashley Polikoff
Photography © 2021 Darren Muir. Food styling by Yolanda Muir. All other illustrations used under license Shutterstock. Author Photo Courtesy of Gigi Boucher.

ISBN: Print 978-1-64876-802-6 | eBook 978-1-64876-228-4
R0

To my family, for always
supporting my crazy dreams.

contents

introduction

Hi! My name is Jen, and I'm happiest when I'm in my kitchen. I am a busy working mom of two, so getting dinner on the table fast is a top priority. I have always believed that a well-stocked pantry is the backbone of the kitchen. With just a simple list of ingredients on hand, you can create a variety of dishes to satisfy your family and friends. Living in the rural Midwest, it's always been important to me to keep a variety of foods on hand in case a blizzard or ice storm makes it impossible to get to the store. Since middle school, I've loved being creative in the kitchen and coming up with new ways to combine these pantry staples. And now, I'm excited to share these recipes with you!

If you're new to pantry cooking, you might be looking for a way to make cooking at home cheaper and easier. Even if you're a seasoned pro, it's easy to feel like you're stuck in a rut of making the same dishes over and over. Either way, I've got your back with the recipes in this book. I'll show you how to stock your pantry and freezer with a limited number of ingredients, and then we'll learn how to turn them into flavorful meals, snacks, and desserts.

In this book, we're defining not only dry goods as pantry staples but also frozen and refrigerated items. It's important to supplement pantry meals with fresh ingredients to add nutrition and variety. And yes, all the recipes in this book can be made solely with the list of ingredients in chapter 1!

Let's get started. I can't wait to show you how simple and delicious pantry cooking can be!

fuss-free pantry cooking

Your pantry is more than your cupboard. When I refer to pantry ingredients, I have in mind much more than shelf-stable dry goods in cans and boxes, as this is an outdated way of thinking about food storage. In this book, you'll find that your pantry actually extends to your freezer and refrigerator. There are so many refrigerated and frozen items that, when stored properly, can keep for months. These ingredients add freshness and variety to the cans and boxes of food on your shelves, combining to create endless dishes.

Cooking from your pantry is all about having a manageable, accessible list of ingredients on hand so you can make a variety of delicious dishes. In this cookbook, we'll be working with 85 staple pantry ingredients.

why cook from your pantry?

Putting together a healthy meal is easy when your pantry is stocked with delicious and nutritious staples like beans, vegetables, spices, stocks, and grains.

> **Variety, please!** – When cooking from a full pantry, you always have something on hand to make and the combinations are endless. No more boring meals on repeat!

> **Nutritious options** – One common misconception is that pantry cooking means lots of processed foods, but I mainly use whole foods and minimally processed ingredients in this book. Cooking healthy meals for your family is easy when you keep the right foods in your kitchen.

> **Save time** – Pantry cooking makes sense for busy home cooks. Once you learn which combinations of foods your family enjoys, it's quick to throw together a meal on hectic weeknights.

> **Cut costs** – Cooking from your pantry cuts food waste and ensures you're getting the most value from your grocery bill. Pantry foods tend to be lower cost and can help keep your food budget in check. Be on the lookout for sales and stock up when items are marked down.

your essential pantry

Welcome to what is arguably the most important section of this cookbook: the list of 85 essential pantry ingredients needed to make every recipe. You are very welcome to keep more ingredients in your personal pantry; however, all the dishes in this book can be made with only these key ingredients—no ifs, ands, or buts.

CUPBOARD CLASSICS

> **Vegetable stock** – This culinary workhorse can be used for so many dishes, including sauces, soups, grains, and gravies. Feel free to use boxed or canned broth as well as bouillon cubes or granules. Chicken stock can also be substituted for any of the recipes in this book. I prefer low-sodium stock or broth so I can control the level of salt in the dish.

> **Mayonnaise** – Shelf-stable until opened, mayonnaise is more than just a spread. Combine it with flaked fish for delicious fish cakes or stir it into cooked chicken or tuna for a quick sandwich filling. Mayo is also ideal as a base for creamy homemade salad dressings.

> **Honey** – A wonderful alternative to white sugar in many recipes, honey can do everything from sweeten up a dressing to serve as a glaze for chicken. It also keeps for years in the pantry.

> **Coconut milk** – This non-dairy hero is often used in curry dishes to provide balance and richness. It can also be whipped with sugar for a non-dairy whipped "cream"—all you need to do is chill the can overnight and scoop off the fat from the top of the can! I prefer full-fat coconut milk for the flavor, but light can also be substituted in most recipes if desired.

> **Olive oil** – Every kitchen should have a bottle of olive oil. It's my go-to when sautéing veggies or meat and is the backbone of many vinaigrettes and marinades. I prefer regular olive oil to extra-virgin, as it can be used in both hot and cold applications.

> **Soy sauce** – This condiment is packed with flavor and has a salty bite. Use it in marinades, sauces, fried rice, and stir-fries for a flavorful kick. Low-sodium soy sauce is my go-to so I can adjust the salt level of dishes on my own.

> **Capers** – This unique ingredient is actually a pickled flower bud that grows in the Mediterranean. Capers provide a nuanced salty taste that is hard to match, and they keep for months in the refrigerator. Be sure to pour off the brine before measuring.

> **Peanut butter** – Not just for PB and J! Keep creamy peanut butter on hand to make a delicious peanut dipping sauce for spring rolls or to stir into an oatmeal cookie recipe. Feel free to use either natural or regular peanut butter in my recipes; just keep in mind that natural peanut butter is not as sweet.

> **Dijon mustard** – This versatile condiment isn't just a sandwich spread. Use Dijon to add a kick to dressings, sauces, and marinades. You can use smooth or whole-grain varieties interchangeably in this book.

> **Sesame oil** – This flavorful oil is a staple in Chinese, Japanese, and Korean dishes. Once opened, store it in the refrigerator to keep it from going rancid.

> **Unseasoned rice vinegar** – This is one of the most versatile vinegars in your pantry. Use it in sauces, salads, and dressings for an acidic kick to balance out

sweet flavors. Rice vinegar has a sweeter and more delicate flavor than other vinegars.

> **Condensed cream of chicken soup** – You might be surprised to find this ingredient on a list of essentials. However, it is a great building block for creamy mains and side dishes.

> **Tomato paste** – Cooked for a few minutes in a skillet, this gives a deep, rich flavor to savory recipes. It can also be combined with water or stock for a smooth tomato sauce.

> **Tahini** — You might not be familiar with tahini, but you can think of it as peanut butter—only made with sesame seeds. Like peanut butter, it can separate, so be sure to stir it before using. It is an integral ingredient in hummus but can also be thinned out to make a dressing for salads or grain bowls.

> **Hot sauce** – There are lots of hot sauces out there, but sriracha is my favorite. Once it's opened, it keeps almost indefinitely in the refrigerator.

> **Walnuts** – You might be most familiar with these in banana bread, but walnuts can also be a welcome addition to salads for extra crunch, protein, and nutrients. Toast raw walnuts in a dry skillet for a stronger flavor.

GRAINS, PASTA, AND NOODLES

> **Dried spaghetti** – This versatile pasta shape can be served with marinara sauce or in a cold noodle salad. Break it into smaller pieces to use in chicken noodle soup.

> **Dried penne** – This short cut noodle is perfect in pasta salads, soups, or with Alfredo sauce.

> **Dried macaroni** – These noodles are great in soups, cold macaroni salad, goulash, or, of course, macaroni and cheese.

> **Farro** – A healthy and pleasantly chewy grain, farro adds texture to salads and grain bowls. It is simple to make and keeps well in the refrigerator once cooked.

> **Brown rice** – I prefer the taste and nutritional content of brown rice to white, and it is arguably one of the most important staples.

> **Rolled oats** – Such a versatile ingredient, oatmeal can be used for everything from cookies to meatballs.

> **Panko bread crumbs** – These have many more uses than plain bread crumbs. They can be used not only as a binder in burgers but also for a crispy breading on fried poultry or fish.

> **Crescent rolls** – These delicious prepared rolls keep in the refrigerator for months and can be used in both sweet and savory dishes. Try them as a crust for a potpie, a quick side for dinner, or a base for a cheese danish.

> **Flour tortillas** – They're not just for tacos! Think enchiladas, quesadillas, burritos, and cold wraps. I typically use white flour tortillas, but whole-wheat can be substituted as well. Six- to eight-inch tortillas are the most versatile size.

> **Corn tortillas** – These can be used for tacos or enchiladas or to thicken tortilla soups. Cut them into triangles and fry them up for quick tortilla chips!

> **Hearty white bread** – Use for sandwiches or paninis or as a binder in meat loaf or meatballs. Bread freezes surprisingly well, but if you still find yourself with stale bread, you can use it for French toast and breakfast casseroles.

LEGUMES AND VEGETABLES

> **Pinto beans** – Arguably the most versatile canned bean, pinto beans can be used in chilis, soups, refried beans, or salads. I usually use regular canned beans, but feel free to use no-salt-added if you're watching your sodium.

> **Chickpeas** – Chickpeas are full of protein and are perfect for whipping up a creamy hummus or adding to cold vegetable salads.

> **Crushed tomatoes** – One of the greatest pantry workhorses, crushed tomatoes can be used in a variety of sauces and soups. Typically, crushed tomatoes and tomato sauce can be used interchangeably.

> **Diced tomatoes** – These add a pop of bright flavor to chilis, stews, or soups. You can even use them as a base for a quick salsa. I prefer petite-diced, but regular varieties can be used as well.

> **Canned corn** – Create a comforting scalloped corn bake or add them to soups, tacos, and salads.

> **Frozen broccoli florets** – Frozen produce is often picked at the peak of freshness and flash frozen, so it tends to retain more of its texture than canned.

> **Frozen shredded potatoes** – Not just for making hash browns, these can be added to a creamy potato soup or folded into a delicious cheesy casserole. Frozen cubed potatoes can also be substituted.

> **Frozen peas** – These versatile veggies defrost quickly and can be added to soups, stews, and cold salads for a pop of green and some plant-based protein.

> **Russet potatoes** – You can prepare baked potatoes for a quick meal, or chop and cook them for perfect mashed potatoes or potato salad.

> **Yellow onions** – These cannot be underestimated as a pantry ingredient. They're inexpensive and add flavor to so many dishes. Be sure to store these separately, as they release moisture and gases that cause potatoes to sprout and spoil more quickly.

> **Garlic** – Fresh garlic perks up almost any dish. Consider investing in a garlic press to finely mince cloves with ease. A zester also works wonderfully to grate them.

CANNED AND FROZEN SEAFOOD

> **Raw frozen shrimp** – These are quick to thaw and can always be kept on hand for an easy stir-fry or pasta dish. Purchase peeled and deveined shrimp to cut down on prep time. Medium or large sizes are the most versatile.

> **Canned tuna** – Although tuna salad sandwiches are great, this versatile and inexpensive fish can also be used in pasta, casseroles, and tuna cakes. I prefer white albacore tuna packed in water, as the flavor is neutral and the pieces of fish tend to be larger.

> **Canned lump crabmeat** – An often-overlooked pantry ingredient, crabmeat can be used in a delicious creamy dip or to make tender and flaky crab cakes.

> **Frozen salmon** – Dice fillets into small pieces for salmon burgers or cook whole fillets for a quick dinner with rice and veggies on the side.

> **Frozen cod** – I prefer the heft and taste of cod, but you can substitute any white fish in your freezer. Be sure not to overcook cod, as it can become tough.

CURED AND FROZEN MEATS

> **Ground beef** – So many recipes can be made with ground beef! I prefer 90 percent lean, but feel free to substitute ground turkey if you prefer.

> **Boneless skinless chicken breasts** – Another freezer mainstay, chicken can be used in so many dishes and keeps for up to six months in the freezer, tightly wrapped.

> Ham – Use it in salads and soups for a salty kick and boost of protein. Combine with beans for a budget-friendly meal or fold into an omelet for breakfast.

> Bacon – Bacon isn't just for breakfast. Use it for BLT sandwiches or crumble it on top of creamy potato soup.

> Pepperoni – Pepperoni keeps well in the refrigerator and can be used to add flavor to sandwiches, salads, or homemade pizza. Pre-sliced pepperoni is the most convenient; feel free to substitute turkey pepperoni if you prefer a lower fat alternative.

> Smoked beef sausage – This sausage freezes well. Sauté it with veggies and rice for a quick dinner or cube it and throw it into an omelet or potato soup.

> Pork loin roast – If you stock up when they're on sale, you can keep pork roasts in the freezer for up to six months, tightly wrapped. Cut a roast into individual pork chops and sauté, or slow cook all day for a comforting dinner.

BAKING STAPLES

> All-purpose flour – Be sure to store it in an airtight container, and it will keep for a long time in your pantry. Use it to thicken soups and sauces or for traditional baked goods.

> White granulated sugar – Another pantry item that keeps well. Use it in traditional baked goods or in sauces, dressings, and marinades. Sugar promotes browning in both sweet and savory dishes and helps balance salty and acidic flavors.

> Brown sugar – This sugar is best for baking or to add a bit of sweetness to chili or curry dishes. I prefer dark brown, but light can be substituted as well.

> Baking powder – This leavening agent is frequently used to help cakes, breads, and muffins rise. It is different from baking soda in that it contains acid. When liquid is added, bubbles form to produce gases and create a fluffy interior.

> Active dry yeast – This magical ingredient can be used to make homemade breads and pizza crust. Remember that active dry yeast must be dissolved in a liquid to activate it prior to mixing.

> Ground cinnamon – A staple for baking, cinnamon adds a spicy warmth to desserts and quick breads.

> Semisweet chocolate chips – Try adding these to cookies, muffins, breads, pancakes, or waffles. I prefer semisweet, as they can be used in a wide array of recipes.

> **Cornmeal** – Did you know you can use cornmeal to make grits? It keeps well in the pantry and can also be used to make corn bread and baked corn casserole. I prefer yellow, stone-ground cornmeal.

> **Vanilla extract** – A must-have for baking, vanilla keeps well in the pantry or spice cabinet for months. Pure and imitation vanilla extract are not the same; opt for pure extract for a tastier vanilla flavor with less additives.

> **Dried cranberries** – These are one of my favorite additions to both baked goods and salads for a pop of tart flavor.

YOUR SPICE RACK

> **Kosher salt** – I much prefer kosher salt to regular iodized salt for cooking. It's easier to sprinkle on foods and allows me to season dishes more accurately. Morton coarse kosher salt is my favorite brand.

> **Black pepper** – Salt's twin can't be left out! I prefer freshly ground pepper, so I purchase whole peppercorns and use a pepper grinder.

> **Chili powder** – Typically, chili powder is a blend of ground chiles, cayenne, cumin, and garlic. Use this spice mixture to season chicken or beef or make your own homemade taco seasoning.

> **Dried dill** – A favorite from the spice cabinet, dill is great in chicken salad and sprinkled on fish before baking. It also pairs well with lemon.

> **Italian seasoning** – This versatile spice mix can be used in more than just Italian dishes. Reach for it any time a recipe calls for oregano or thyme.

> **Garam masala** – This is a warm Indian spice blend that is great in curry dishes. It typically includes cumin, coriander, cardamom, pepper, cinnamon, cloves, and nutmeg.

> **Cumin** – This is another versatile spice that is used in a variety of cuisines, from Tex-Mex to Indian.

> **Cayenne pepper** – A little goes a long way! Use this spice to kick up any dish.

> **Turmeric** – This lovely yellow spice adds color and warm flavor to soups, curries, and stews.

> **Paprika** – This colorful spice adds a subtle flavor and a rich red color to many dishes.

STORING YOUR STAPLES

Use this handy cheat sheet for a general idea of how long you can hang on to your pantry staples, as well as ideal storage conditions.

INGREDIENT	STORAGE INSTRUCTIONS	HOW LONG WILL IT KEEP?
Canned stock and soup	In a cool, dry cupboard	3–5 years unopened
Mayonnaise	Refrigerate once opened	2 months once opened
Honey	In a cool, dry cupboard	Years (honey does not expire)
Canned coconut milk	In a cool, dry cupboard	2–5 years unopened
Soy sauce	Refrigerate once opened	2 years
Mustard	Refrigerate once opened	1 year
Hot sauce	Refrigerate once opened	3 years
Capers (brined)	Refrigerate once opened	1 year
Peanut butter	In a cool, dry cupboard	3–4 months once opened
Sesame oil	Refrigerate once opened	6–8 months once opened
Olive oil	In a cool, dry cupboard	2–4 years
Rice vinegar	In a cool, dry cupboard	3–5 years
Tahini	Refrigerate once opened	6 months once opened
Canned tomato products	In a cool, dry cupboard	2 years
Dried pasta, rice, and grains	In a cool, dry cupboard	3–5 years
Rolled oats	In a cool, dry cupboard	1–2 years
Bread crumbs	In a cool, dry cupboard (refrigerate if in a humid climate)	1 year
Crescent rolls	Refrigerate	Use by date on can
Flour and corn tortillas	Refrigerate or freeze once opened	2–4 weeks refrigerated; 3 months frozen
Dried nuts	In a cool, dry cupboard (refrigerate or freeze if in a hot climate)	6–12 months in pantry; 1–2 years refrigerated or frozen
Bread	Freeze if not eaten by date on package	3–6 months frozen
Canned beans/legumes	In a cool, dry cupboard	3–5 years
Canned vegetables	In a cool, dry cupboard	3–5 years
Frozen vegetables	Frozen and tightly wrapped	1–2 years
Potatoes, onions, garlic	In a cool, dry cupboard, stored apart	2–4 weeks depending on the temperature and humidity (keeps longer if kept cool)
Frozen seafood	Frozen and tightly wrapped	1 year
Canned seafood	In a cool, dry cupboard	3–5 years
Frozen meat, pork, or poultry	Frozen and tightly wrapped	4–12 months
Dry baking goods	In a cool, dry cupboard	6–12 months
Dry spices and seasonings	In a cool, dry cupboard	2–4 years

15 fresh ingredients to keep on your list

For variety's sake, you can't live on pantry goods alone. There are some fresh foods that just don't have a great pantry substitute, such as eggs, dairy, and fresh vegetables. Here are the 15 fresh ingredients that will be used in the recipes throughout this book.

> **Green leaf lettuce** – Properly washed and dried, lettuce can last a week in the refrigerator. Use it to top tacos, liven up a sandwich, or even make a hearty entrée salad.

> **Carrots** – These will last quite a while if kept dry and refrigerated. Use them to add sweetness to soups or grate them on top of a sandwich or salad.

> **Lemons** – Citrus fruits keep for weeks in the refrigerator. Use the zest to liven up baked goods and the juice to bring a tart acidity to dressings and marinades.

> **Limes** – Lemons' tangy cousins, limes are also a great staple to keep on hand for adding to dressings and finishing dishes.

> **Cilantro** – This herb's bright, aromatic flavor helps bring fresh flavor and vibrant color to dishes. If you're cilantro-averse, substitute flat-leaf parsley.

> **Bananas** – While these make a great snack, they are also a healthy sweetener in pancakes, muffins, and quick breads.

> **Apples** – These will last weeks in the refrigerator. Cut them up for a quick snack or add them to salads and desserts.

> **Cheddar cheese** – A sharp yellow cheddar is an amazingly versatile cheese. Use it to top a sandwich, salad, or any dish that could use a bit of richness. Blocks of cheese tend to be the most useful, as you can shred them yourself, cut slices for a sandwich, or make cubes for a salad.

> **Mozzarella cheese** – This gooey melting cheese is great in Italian pasta bakes, on top of pizza, or tucked into a calzone. I prefer part-skim shredded mozzarella, as it is easy to use and the most versatile.

> **Parmesan cheese** – This sharp and salty cheese is a welcome addition to soups and pasta dishes.

> **Sour cream** – Use this creamy topping in dressings and casseroles or to top tacos. Sour cream can also be used to tame a particularly spicy dish.

> **Cream cheese** – Did you know that cream cheese can be frozen for up to three months? The texture may be affected, so once thawed, use it in a hot dish like a casserole rather than a cold cream cheese frosting.

> **Eggs** – Used for both sweet and savory dishes alike, eggs are an inexpensive way to add protein to a meal. All the recipes in this book call for large eggs.

> **Butter** – Unsalted butter is another kitchen workhorse. Use it to add richness to savory dishes or in desserts and muffins.

> **Milk** – I prefer whole milk for cooking, but any milk can be substituted.

GET CREATIVE!

Pantry cooking can get a bit repetitive, but there are lots of ways to use your basic ingredients in unexpected ways. Here are some ideas:

> Have a bit of dried potato flakes in the bottom of the box? Use them to thicken up a soup or a stew. I do this often with Classic Potato Soup (page 29) and it works great!

> Make a delicious peanut vinaigrette to serve with fresh salad by using the last few tablespoons of a jar of peanut butter. Bonus: You can make it right in the jar without dirtying a dish!

> Out of bread crumbs for your meat loaf? Pulse some crackers, cornflakes, or dried oats in a food processor for a quick binding agent.

> Canned coconut milk is a pantry jack-of-all-trades: Use it in savory stews and curries, add it to your smoothie at breakfast, or even whip it up for a dairy-free dessert topping!

> Have bits of dried fruit, chocolate chips, or nuts in your pantry? Make a crispy granola that's great with yogurt or on its own as a hearty cereal.

ORGANIZING YOUR ESSENTIALS

I know I've been there, and I'm sure you have, too—digging out a package of freezer-burned meat or biting into a rancid nut isn't fun. Here are some tips for organization so you can more easily find what you have and keep food from going bad.

> Repackage foods into clear containers. Label them and include the expiration date on each container to ensure you know when to use the food by. Clear containers make it easy to see what you have, which can also inspire you to cook with those ingredients.

> Always label any freezer bag with the contents! One of the biggest lies I tell myself is that I'll remember what's in the bag.

> Keep a permanent marker in a drawer or on a string in your pantry. Removing the hassle of searching for a marker makes it much quicker to label containers or freezer bags.

> Consider keeping a running list on paper or use an app on your smartphone to track your pantry inventory.

> Designate a week or two out of every year dedicated to pantry meals. Consider it a challenge to use what you have and make fewer trips to the store.

top tips for pantry stocking and meal planning

One of the best feelings is looking in your kitchen and seeing a well-stocked array of ingredients just waiting to be combined into a delicious meal. Once you get the hang of shopping and planning, the work of stocking a pantry will mean fewer emergency trips to the store and less money spent.

> **Take stock of the ingredients in your pantry, freezer, and refrigerator.** Before going to the grocery store, evaluate what you already have on hand and think about what dishes you can make with minimal additions from the store.

> **Check expiration dates.** Got something that's about to expire? Make a plan to use it up for that week's meals to avoid food waste.

> **Keep track of your supply.** Maintain a whiteboard or paper list in your kitchen where you write down pantry ingredients when you use them up. This will help you remember to replace them during your next shopping trip.

> **Don't overbuy just because it's on sale.** If there is a great deal at the store but you can't use it all, it's still food and money wasted. Know the ingredients that you use frequently and that your household enjoys, and stick to those.

> **Consider bulk shopping for dried staples such as rice and beans.** You can often get a cheaper price in bulk, and these ingredients will keep for years in your pantry.

essential pantry cooking gear

If you're a regular home cook, you probably have everything you need to make the recipes in this book. Here are some of the tools you'll want to have on hand:

> Sharp knives, including a paring knife, bread knife, and chef's knife

> Rubber spatula

> Silicone spatula for turning meats and fish

> Wooden spoon

> Whisk

> Tongs

> Nonstick skillet

> Saucepan

> Pasta pot

> Baking sheets

> 9-by-13-inch baking dish

> Food processor or blender

> Box grater

> Garlic press

> Zester

> Mixing bowls of various sizes

about the recipes

All of the main recipes in this book can be made with the 70 pantry essentials and 15 fresh ingredients listed in this chapter—nothing else needed. Each chapter is organized by the type of ingredient, which mirrors the categories of pantry staples starting on page 2. You can also find recipes by using the index in the back of this book (page 132).

BLUEPRINT RECIPES

Blueprint recipes are flexible outlines that allow you to substitute what you have on hand. These still only use the 85 ingredients listed in this chapter; however, they also offer other ingredient variations. Feel free to make these recipes your own and switch up the flavor combinations to keep mealtimes exciting. These are marked in blue text in the recipe lists at the beginning of each chapter.

RECIPE RIFFS

Get creative! Recipe riffs are a departure from the core 85 ingredients and allow you to make substitutions to incorporate variety. You'll find 100 of them in this book—they're located underneath the recipes.

RECIPE TIPS AND LABELS

> **Cooking tip:** A tip for prepping or cooking a dish that provides a suggestion or specific instruction on how to work with an ingredient.

> **Reinvent it:** A tip explaining how to transform leftovers into a completely new dish.

> **In a pinch:** A tip for substituting a similar ingredient, either for another pantry ingredient or a fresh ingredient.

> **Storage tip:** Information on storing the recipe once it's prepared and the best way to do so.

This book also includes dietary labels for your convenience: vegetarian, vegan, gluten-free, and dairy-free. When you're cooking for anyone with a dietary restriction or sensitivity, remember to double-check the ingredients lists of all your products to be sure they don't contain unexpected additives.

Ready? Let's cook!

Perfect Piecrust, page 30

cupboard classics

In this chapter, you will find recipes for dressings, marinades, sauces, and soups that serve as the building blocks of subsequent recipes throughout this book. Made with minimal ingredients, they illustrate the versatility of basic pantry staples. Quick pasta sauces, such as marinara, Alfredo, and a simple cheese sauce, make it easy to create a comforting pasta dinner. Baked Brown Rice, Stir-Fry Sauce, and a variety of salad dressings are great to have in the refrigerator for meal prep. Mastering these basics provides a road map to pantry cooking success!

simple vinaigrette

DAIRY-FREE · GLUTEN-FREE · VEGETARIAN

YIELD: 1½ CUPS

PREP: 10 MINUTES

½ cup vinegar:

- Apple cider vinegar
- Rice wine vinegar
- Balsamic vinegar
- Red wine vinegar

3½ tablespoons liquid sweetener:

- Honey
- Maple syrup
- Agave nectar

¼ cup lemon juice

4 garlic cloves, minced

¾ teaspoon Italian seasoning

½ teaspoon dried dill

½ teaspoon kosher salt

¼ teaspoon freshly ground black pepper

¾ cup oil:

- Olive oil
- Avocado oil
- Canola oil

Homemade vinaigrettes taste so much better than bottled! This versatile salad dressing can be made quickly with ingredients you likely have in your pantry. Fresh herbs also make a lovely addition if you happen to have any on hand. Try this vinaigrette over a salad of greens and other vegetables or as a dressing for a pasta salad.

1 In a bowl, whisk together the vinegar, sweetener, lemon juice, garlic, Italian seasoning, dill, salt, and pepper. Slowly whisk in the oil to emulsify and combine.

2 Alternatively, shake all the ingredients together in a jar with a tight-fitting lid. I prefer this method because the jar doubles as a storage vessel. Shake or whisk again before serving.

RECIPE RIFFS

Cilantro-Lime Vinaigrette: Use rice wine vinegar in the recipe and substitute the juice and zest of 1 lime for the lemon juice. Omit the Italian seasoning and dill, and add ¼ cup of fresh chopped cilantro.

Feta Vinaigrette: Follow the recipe using red wine vinegar. Omit the Italian seasoning and add 2 tablespoons of finely minced fresh parsley and ⅓ cup of crumbled feta cheese.

COOKING TIP: Vinaigrette is a great make-ahead item. Use it as a salad dressing for quick lunches throughout the week or for an easy side salad with dinner. Try tossing it with cold cooked pasta, leftover vegetables, and chickpeas for a quick meal prep. If you're using fresh herbs instead of dried, a good rule of thumb is to triple the amount.

STORAGE TIP: Vinaigrettes will keep for up to 2 weeks in the refrigerator.

REINVENT IT: Leftover vinaigrette works great as a marinade for chicken or steak.

creamy salad dressing, three ways

GLUTEN-FREE · VEGETARIAN

YIELD: 2 CUPS

PREP: 10 MINUTES

BASE DRESSING INGREDIENTS

1 cup mayonnaise

½ cup sour cream

½ cup milk

2 tablespoons lemon juice

1 teaspoon kosher salt

¼ teaspoon freshly ground black pepper

RANCH DRESSING

1½ teaspoons dried dill

¼ teaspoon paprika

1 garlic clove, minced

CREAMY GARLIC DRESSING

2 teaspoons Dijon mustard

1 teaspoon unseasoned rice vinegar

1 teaspoon granulated sugar

2 garlic cloves, minced

CILANTRO-LIME DRESSING

Juice and zest of 1 lime

¼ teaspoon ground cumin

¼ cup fresh cilantro, minced

1 garlic clove, minced

A big salad packed with protein and topped with a homemade creamy salad dressing makes for a satisfying meal. Surprisingly, most creamy dressings share the same base ingredients with just a few changes in seasonings. These versatile dressing recipes can also be used as dips for fresh vegetables, and the Cilantro-Lime Dressing is perfect for drizzling over tacos.

1 In a bowl, whisk together all of the base dressing ingredients until well combined.

2 Stir in the additional ingredients for the specific dressing you're making.

RECIPE RIFFS

Blue Cheese Dressing: Make Ranch Dressing recipe as directed, then stir in ½ cup of blue cheese crumbles.

Chipotle-Ranch Dressing: Make the recipe as directed, then stir in 1 tablespoon of diced chipotle in adobo sauce and ½ teaspoon of ground cumin.

COOKING TIP: Dressings are a great make-ahead item. Use them as a salad dressing for quick lunches throughout the week or to dress a side salad for dinner. Serve with raw vegetables for a quick appetizer or lunch box item for your kids.

STORAGE TIP: These dairy-based dressings will keep for up to a week in the refrigerator, tightly covered. Stir well before serving.

the absolute best marinade

DAIRY-FREE · VEGETARIAN

YIELD: 1¼ CUPS

PREP: 10 MINUTES

⅓ cup vinegar:

- Rice wine vinegar
- Apple cider vinegar
- Balsamic vinegar

½ cup soy sauce

2 tablespoons liquid sweetener:

- Honey
- Maple syrup
- Agave nectar

2 tablespoons Dijon mustard

4 garlic cloves, minced

2 teaspoons Italian seasoning

½ teaspoon freshly ground black pepper

¼ cup oil:

- Olive oil
- Avocado oil
- Canola oil

I developed this marinade recipe after a disappointing summer spent grilling lots of flavorless chicken breasts. Never again! The best part is that this marinade is so versatile, you can use it on nearly everything. Try it with beef, chicken, vegetable kebabs, tofu, or fish.

1 In a bowl, whisk together the vinegar, soy sauce, sweetener, mustard, garlic, Italian seasoning, and pepper. Slowly whisk in the oil to emulsify and combine. Alternatively, shake all the ingredients together in a jar with a tight-fitting lid.

2 Pour into a shallow dish and add your desired protein or vegetables, turning to coat.

3 For beef, chicken, vegetables, or tofu, marinate for at least an hour but not more than 24 hours. For fish, marinate for at least 30 minutes but not more than 2 hours. This recipe will make enough marinade for 4 to 6 portions of protein, tofu, or vegetables.

COOKING TIP: Gallon-size zip-top bags are great for marinating foods since you can squeeze most of the air out to ensure that the marinade has direct contact with the protein. To prevent burning, pat food dry before cooking, especially if cooking over high heat.

STORAGE TIP: This marinade can be made ahead and will last for up to 2 weeks in the refrigerator, tightly covered.

IN A PINCH: You can substitute ⅓ cup of Worcestershire sauce for the soy sauce if you don't have any on hand.

peanut sauce

DAIRY-FREE · VEGAN

YIELD: 1 CUP

PREP: 10 MINUTES

⅓ cup creamy peanut butter

¼ cup hot water, plus more as needed

3 tablespoons lime juice

2 tablespoons soy sauce

2 tablespoons chopped fresh cilantro

1 garlic clove, minced

1 teaspoon sesame oil

½ teaspoon hot sauce

This savory, delicious sauce can be made in a matter of minutes! Try using it as a dip for spring rolls or grilled chicken, thinning it out with a little water to use as a dressing, or tossing it with cold noodles and veggies for a refreshing salad.

In a bowl, whisk together all the ingredients until well combined. Add more hot water 1 tablespoon at a time to thin the sauce, if needed.

RECIPE RIFFS

Thai-Style Chicken Wraps: In a tortilla or wrap, layer leftover grilled chicken, lettuce, cucumber, bell pepper, and cilantro and roll up tightly. Cut into pinwheels and dip in Peanut Sauce for a tasty lunch.

Chicken with Peanut Sauce: Warm the finished sauce in a small saucepan over medium heat until heated through. Drizzle over cooked chicken breast and Baked Brown Rice (page 32).

STORAGE TIP: Peanut Sauce will keep in the refrigerator for up to 2 weeks, tightly covered.

alfredo sauce

VEGETARIAN

YIELD: 2¾ CUPS
PREP: 5 MINUTES
COOK: 10 MINUTES

4 tablespoons unsalted butter

2 garlic cloves, minced

2 tablespoons all-purpose flour

½ teaspoon kosher salt

4 ounces cream cheese, room temperature

2 cups milk

1½ cups grated Parmesan cheese

¼ teaspoon freshly ground black pepper

If you've never made homemade Alfredo sauce before, give this recipe a try. It is so much richer and creamier than the jarred kind! Cream cheese isn't a traditional ingredient in Alfredo, but it helps thicken the sauce here. This also makes a fabulous dip for breadsticks or a non-traditional pizza sauce.

1   In a saucepan, melt the butter over medium-low heat. Add the garlic and cook for 1 to 2 minutes, until fragrant. Whisk in the flour and salt.

2   Add the cream cheese and cook until melted, stirring frequently.

3   Whisk in the milk, Parmesan cheese, and pepper. Continue to cook over medium heat, whisking frequently until combined, about 5 minutes.

RECIPE RIFFS

Chicken and Broccoli Alfredo: Combine the finished sauce with cooked penne pasta, cubed cooked chicken, and steamed broccoli florets for a filling meal.

Cajun-Inspired Alfredo with Shrimp or Chicken: Follow the recipe as directed, then stir 2 teaspoons of Cajun seasoning into the finished sauce. Serve with hot cooked pasta and sautéed chicken or shrimp.

STORAGE TIP: This recipe is best served fresh; however, it can be refrigerated for up to 5 days. To reheat the sauce, warm it in a pan over medium heat, adding milk to thin if needed. You can also reheat the sauce in the microwave.

marinara sauce

DAIRY-FREE · GLUTEN-FREE · VEGAN

YIELD: **3 CUPS**

PREP: **5 MINUTES**

COOK: **10 MINUTES**

2 tablespoons olive oil

½ yellow onion, chopped

3 garlic cloves, minced

1 (28-ounce) can crushed tomatoes

2 teaspoons Italian seasoning

1 teaspoon kosher salt

1 teaspoon granulated sugar

If I had to choose just one pantry ingredient to keep on hand, it would be canned tomatoes. They bring flavor to so many recipes, and by adding a few simple ingredients, you can make a delicious marinara sauce in no time at all. Try it as a basic pasta sauce or as a dipping sauce for Pepperoni Rolls (page 122).

1 In a large skillet, heat the oil over medium heat. Add the onion and sauté for 3 to 4 minutes, until translucent.

2 Add the garlic and cook for about 1 minute, just until fragrant.

3 Carefully pour in the crushed tomatoes and stir in the Italian seasoning, salt, and sugar. Cook over medium-low heat for 5 minutes, stirring occasionally. If the sauce gets too thick, add hot water in 2-tablespoon increments to thin.

4 Remove from the heat and adjust the seasoning to taste by adding more salt, sugar, or Italian seasoning to balance the flavors.

RECIPE RIFFS

Spicy Sausage Marinara: Add 8 ounces of cooked and crumbled Italian sausage and 1 teaspoon of red pepper flakes to the finished sauce.

Easy Chicken Cacciatore: Cut 2 boneless skinless chicken breasts into bite-size pieces and season with salt and pepper. Dice 1 bell pepper and ⅓ cup of pitted Kalamata olives. Follow the recipe, sautéing the chicken and pepper with the onion in step 1 until the chicken is cooked through. Stir in the olives, then continue with the recipe as directed.

Parma Rosa Sauce: Follow the recipe as directed. After removing the sauce from the heat, stir in ¼ cup of heavy (whipping) cream and ⅓ cup of grated Parmesan cheese.

COOKING TIP: Canned tomatoes can vary in sweetness depending on the brand, type of tomato, or time of year harvested. Because of this, be sure to always taste the finished sauce and adjust the seasoning as desired.

STORAGE TIP: Store the prepared sauce in the refrigerator for up to 5 days. You can also freeze the sauce in an airtight container for up to 3 months.

stir-fry sauce

DAIRY-FREE · VEGETARIAN

YIELD: 2 CUPS

PREP: 10 MINUTES

1 tablespoon all-purpose flour

1 tablespoon sesame oil

1 cup vegetable stock

⅓ cup water

3 tablespoons unseasoned rice vinegar

⅓ cup soy sauce

3 tablespoons brown sugar

2 garlic cloves, minced

1 teaspoon hot sauce

This magical sauce can help you whip up a week-night dinner super quick! Keep some on hand along with precut vegetables and protein in the refrigerator and you're 20 minutes away from a delicious dinner. Check out my Quick and Easy Stir-Fry (page 97) for a blueprint of how to cook with this sauce.

1 In a medium bowl, whisk together the flour and sesame oil until well combined.

2 Whisk in the vegetable stock, water, rice vinegar, soy sauce, brown sugar, garlic, and hot sauce.

> **STORAGE TIP:** This sauce will keep in the refrigerator for up to 2 weeks, tightly covered.

basic cheese sauce

VEGETARIAN

YIELD: 2 CUPS

PREP: 5 MINUTES

COOK: 10 MINUTES

2 tablespoons unsalted butter

2 tablespoons all-purpose flour

1 teaspoon kosher salt

½ teaspoon granulated sugar

¼ teaspoon freshly ground black pepper

2 cups milk

1 teaspoon Dijon mustard

2 cups shredded cheddar cheese

This simple cheese sauce is based on a classic French sauce of butter, flour, and milk called béchamel. Try this recipe as the base for baked macaroni and cheese, or serve it over baked potatoes or steamed broccoli as a flavorful sauce. You can even add Speedy Salsa (page 28) and turn it into queso!

1 In a heavy-bottomed skillet, melt the butter over medium heat. Whisk in the flour, salt, sugar, and pepper and cook for 1 to 2 minutes, until bubbling.

2 Whisk in the milk and mustard. Cook the sauce, whisking frequently, for 3 to 5 more minutes, or until thickened. Remove from the heat and add the shredded cheese, whisking until melted. Serve immediately.

RECIPE RIFFS

Baked Macaroni and Cheese: Boil 2 cups of macaroni pasta for 8 to 10 minutes, or according to the package directions. Drain. Fold the cooked pasta into the cheese sauce, then pour the mixture into a baking dish. Top with additional shredded cheese and bake at 400°F for 15 minutes, or until bubbling.

Beer Cheese Dip: Follow the recipe as directed, substituting 1 cup of milk for 1 cup of light beer and increasing the mustard to 1 tablespoon. Serve with soft pretzels or sautéed sliced kielbasa.

STORAGE TIP: This sauce is best made right before serving and does not freeze well.

REINVENT IT: Try reheating leftover cheese sauce the next morning and adding it to a breakfast burrito or drizzling it over an egg and potato scramble.

speedy salsa

DAIRY-FREE · GLUTEN-FREE · VEGAN

YIELD: 3 CUPS

PREP: 10 MINUTES,
PLUS 2 HOURS TO CHILL

1 (28-ounce) can diced
   tomatoes, undrained

½ yellow onion, chopped

½ cup fresh cilantro

2 garlic cloves, minced

Juice of 1 lime

2 teaspoons hot sauce

½ teaspoon kosher salt

½ teaspoon granulated
   sugar

½ teaspoon ground cumin

¼ teaspoon freshly ground
   black pepper

Making salsa couldn't be simpler when you start with canned diced tomatoes and let a food processor do the work for you. It's so easy and tastes much fresher than the jarred kind. Try this salsa as an accompaniment to chips, tacos, nachos, or enchiladas.

1 In a food processor or blender, combine all the ingredients and pulse to the desired consistency. Be careful not to puree it, or you'll have more of a picante sauce than a chunky salsa. Taste and adjust the seasonings.

2 Pour the salsa into a medium bowl and refrigerate, covered, for at least 2 hours before serving.

RECIPE RIFFS

Queso Dip: In a saucepan, combine 1½ cups of salsa with 16 ounces of cubed American cheese and cook over low heat until melted, stirring often. Serve with tortilla chips.

Corn and Black Bean Salsa: Stir 1 cup each of rinsed and drained black beans and canned corn into the completed salsa.

STORAGE TIP: Homemade salsa will keep for up to 5 days in the refrigerator. Salsa can also be frozen for up to 3 months; the texture may be affected but the quality will not.

classic potato soup

VEGETARIAN

YIELD: 6 SERVINGS

PREP: 15 MINUTES

COOK: 30 MINUTES

4 tablespoons unsalted butter

1 medium yellow onion, diced

1 carrot, peeled and diced

2 garlic cloves, minced

4 russet potatoes, peeled and cubed

4 cups vegetable stock

3 cups milk

¼ cup all-purpose flour

2 teaspoons kosher salt

½ teaspoon freshly ground black pepper

This potato soup is one of the first recipes I learned to cook when I moved out on my own. It's simple, delicious, and can be customized with a variety of toppings. My favorite way to serve it is with ham and biscuits. I also love it topped with shredded cheddar cheese, sliced scallions, and crumbled bacon. This soup makes great leftovers and is very filling.

1 In a large pot, melt the butter over medium heat. Add the onion, carrot, and garlic and cook for 6 to 8 minutes, until tender.

2 Add the potatoes and vegetable stock. Cover the pot, leaving the lid slightly ajar, and bring to a boil. Continue to cook over medium-high heat for 15 to 20 minutes, until the potatoes are tender.

3 In a medium bowl, whisk together the milk and flour until smooth. Reduce the heat to medium-low and slowly add the milk-and-flour mixture to the pot, stirring constantly. Stir in the salt and pepper and simmer until thickened.

4 Remove from the heat and adjust the seasoning to taste. Top as desired before serving.

COOKING TIP: If the soup needs additional thickening, adding dried potato flakes works great!

RECIPE RIFFS

Ham and Cheddar Potato Soup: Add diced cooked ham and shredded cheddar cheese to the finished soup.

Potato-Leek Soup: Prepare the soup as directed, substituting the onion and carrot for 2 sliced leeks. Be sure to wash the leeks carefully after slicing since the insides collect grit as they grow.

perfect piecrust

VEGETARIAN

YIELD: 1 SINGLE PIECRUST

PREP: 15 MINUTES, PLUS 30 MINUTES TO CHILL

2 cups all-purpose flour

1 teaspoon kosher salt

11 tablespoons cold unsalted butter

¼ cup ice water, plus more as needed

½ teaspoon unseasoned rice vinegar

Piecrust is a versatile component of both sweet and savory dishes, and it's easier to make than you might think. However, dough is subject to the humidity of the environment, so use your best judgement and add more flour or water if needed. Homemade piecrust is so flaky and delicious, once you get the hang of it, you'll never buy a prepared crust again!

1 Sift the flour and salt into a food processor or large bowl. Cut the cold butter into small cubes.

2 Process the flour mixture with the butter until the pieces of butter are the size of small peas. Alternatively, cut the butter into the flour mixture using a pastry cutter.

3 Mix the ice water (ensure no chunks of ice are present) with the rice vinegar. Slowly stir the water and vinegar mixture into the flour mixture until all the flour is moistened and the dough forms into a ball.

4 Wrap the dough ball tightly in plastic wrap. Refrigerate the dough for at least 30 minutes before using, though it can be refrigerated for up to 2 days.

5 When ready to use, roll the dough out on a floured surface and use as the recipe directs. To blind-bake the crust, preheat the oven to 425°F. Place the crust in a 9-inch pie plate, then top with foil or parchment paper and pour in pie weights or dried beans. Bake for 8 to 10 minutes.

Cinnamon Crisps: Cut the rolled-out dough into strips with a pizza cutter or cut out shapes with cookie cutters. Place the cut dough on a baking sheet, brush it with melted butter, and sprinkle cinnamon sugar over the top. Bake at 425° for 6 to 9 minutes, until golden brown. This is a great way to use up spare scraps of crust!

STORAGE TIP: Prepared, unbaked piecrust can be refrigerated for up to 2 days or frozen for up to 3 months. Ensure it is wrapped tightly to avoid flavor transfer from other items. Thaw frozen piecrust in the refrigerator before using.

COOKING TIP: This recipe makes enough for a single-crust pie. Double it if you're making a pie with both a top and bottom crust.

baked brown rice

GLUTEN-FREE · VEGETARIAN

YIELD: **5 CUPS**

PREP: **5 MINUTES, PLUS 5 MINUTES TO STAND**

COOK: **1 HOUR**

2 cups uncooked brown rice

2 tablespoons unsalted butter

1 teaspoon kosher salt

3⅓ cups boiling water

Rice is one of those basic staples that can be hard to master on the stovetop—get the heat wrong, and you'll end up with either a raw or scorched pot of rice. Baking rice in the oven is so simple and turns out perfect every time! I use brown rice here because it is a bit healthier than the white variety, and I enjoy the extra flavor and firmer texture.

1 Preheat the oven to 375°F. Place the rice in a 9-by-13-inch oven-safe dish with the butter and salt.

2 Pour the boiling water over the rice. Stir to combine, melting the butter and mixing it into the rice. Spread into an even layer.

3 Cover the dish tightly with foil and bake for 1 hour.

4 Remove from the oven and fluff with a fork. Allow to stand, uncovered, for 5 minutes before serving.

RECIPE RIFFS

Cilantro-Lime Rice: After the rice is cooked, stir in the juice of 2 limes and ½ cup of chopped fresh cilantro.

Lemony Edamame Rice: After the rice is cooked, stir in the juice of 1 lemon and 1 cup of cooked and shelled edamame.

STORAGE TIP: Cooked rice will keep for up to 5 days in the refrigerator or can be frozen in an airtight container for up to 3 months.

COOKING TIP: To make this recipe vegan, omit the butter or use an equal amount of olive oil instead. Either way, do not skip the last step of allowing the rice to stand. This helps the rice become fluffy.

grains, pasta, and noodles

In this chapter, you'll find a variety of recipes using grain-based pantry staples that are delicious and filling, yet simple to put together. I'll share recipes you can prepare ahead of time for easy weeknight meals, like Peanut Noodle Salad and Enchiladas with Red Sauce. You'll also find options that are ideal for lunches or lighter dinners as well, including Nourishing Grain Bowls and Vegetable Fried Rice. From salad to curry to goulash, the dishes in this chapter are sure to please even picky palates and are perfect for family dinners.

farro waldorf salad

VEGETARIAN

SERVES 4

PREP: 10 MINUTES

COOK: 25 MINUTES

1 cup uncooked farro

⅓ cup mayonnaise

¼ cup sour cream

2 tablespoons unseasoned
rice vinegar

1 tablespoon honey

1 tablespoon lemon juice

1 tablespoon dried dill

1 teaspoon kosher salt

¼ teaspoon freshly ground
black pepper

2 apples, cored and diced

1 cup walnuts, chopped

⅓ cup dried cranberries

If you've never tried farro, you're in for a treat. It's a delicious, chewy grain that can be served hot or cold and makes a great addition to salads. In this recipe, farro makes my modern take on the classic Waldorf salad more filling and adds texture.

1 Bring a pot of water to boil and cook the farro for 20 to 25 minutes, or according to package directions. Drain and rinse briefly with cold water.

2 In a large bowl, whisk together the mayonnaise, sour cream, vinegar, honey, lemon juice, dill, salt, and pepper. Stir in the cooled farro.

3 Add in the apples, walnuts, and cranberries. Stir and adjust the seasoning to taste.

RECIPE RIFF

Arugula and Farro Salad: Omit the apples and cranberries. Instead, add 1 cup of halved cherry tomatoes and ⅓ cup of sliced radishes. Serve on a bed of arugula and top with chopped fresh parsley.

STORAGE TIP: This salad gets better as it sits. You can store it in the refrigerator for up to 3 days.

REINVENT IT: Add grilled chicken to this salad and serve it in large leaves of lettuce or whole-wheat tortillas.

quick quesadillas

VEGETARIAN

SERVES 4

PREP: 15 MINUTES

COOK: 20 MINUTES

8 (8-inch) flour tortillas

2 tablespoons unsalted butter, melted

2 to 3 cups cooked protein:

- Filling from Spicy Beef and Potato Tacos (page 43)
- Cooked chicken, shredded or cubed
- Canned black or pinto beans, rinsed and drained

2 cups shredded cheese:

- Cheddar
- Pepper Jack
- Monterey Jack

Sour cream, salsa, and fresh chopped cilantro, for serving

Quesadillas are one of the quickest meals to get on the table on a busy weeknight, and they are perfect for picky eaters. This recipe is so versatile and can be customized to suit whatever ingredients (or choosy palates) you have on hand. For an extra quick meal, prep the fillings in advance and simply assemble and heat the quesadillas at mealtime.

1 Preheat a large nonstick skillet over medium heat.

2 Brush one side of each tortilla with the melted butter. Place a tortilla, buttered-side down, in the skillet and top it with ½ cup of protein and ½ cup of cheese. Place another tortilla on top, buttered-side up.

3 Cook over medium heat until brown and crispy. Flip and continue cooking until the other side is also browned. Repeat with the remaining tortillas, cheese, and protein.

4 Cut the quesadillas into quarters and serve with sour cream, salsa, and cilantro.

RECIPE RIFF

Philly Cheesesteak Quesadillas: Fill the quesadillas with cooked ground beef, sautéed green peppers, and shredded Swiss cheese and cook as directed.

COOKING TIP: Patience is key with quesadillas. Cook them over medium heat for the crispiest texture, and be sure to keep an eye on them since they burn quickly!

seven-layer pasta salad

SERVES 6 TO 8

PREP: 25 MINUTES

COOK: 15 MINUTES

2 cups dried macaroni

2 teaspoons olive oil

4 large eggs

1 cup mayonnaise

½ cup sour cream

1 tablespoon Dijon mustard

½ teaspoon dried dill

Kosher salt

Freshly ground black pepper

3 cups shredded green leaf lettuce

1 cup cooked ham, diced

½ cup pepperoni, diced

1 (10-ounce) package frozen peas, thawed

1½ cups shredded cheddar cheese

This recipe is an updated take on the classic seven-layer salad from the 1950s. It can be made ahead of time and is a great dish to bring to a gathering or serve as a quick lunch throughout the week. For a beautiful presentation, layer the ingredients in a clear glass trifle dish.

1 Bring a large pot of salted water to a boil and add the macaroni. Cook for about 8 minutes, until al dente or according to the package directions. Drain and rinse with cold water. Toss with the oil and set aside.

2 Place the eggs in a saucepan and cover them with cold water. Bring to a boil, then cover and turn off the heat. Let sit for 15 minutes, then rinse the eggs under cold water and peel them. Slice the eggs and set aside.

3 In a medium bowl, whisk together the mayonnaise, sour cream, mustard, and dill. Season to taste with salt and pepper and set aside.

4 Arrange the lettuce in a serving dish or bowl. Top with the macaroni, then the sliced eggs. Sprinkle with salt and pepper.

5 Layer the ham and pepperoni on top of the eggs, then add the peas. Top with dressing and cheddar just before serving.

COOKING TIP: The dressing and hard-boiled eggs can be prepared ahead of time and stored in the refrigerator. You can also layer this salad in individual serving dishes or meal prep containers.

vegetable fried rice

DAIRY-FREE · VEGETARIAN

SERVES 4

PREP: 10 MINUTES

COOK: 20 MINUTES

3 tablespoons olive oil, divided

½ medium onion, diced

2 carrots, peeled and diced

2 cups frozen peas, thawed

4 garlic cloves, minced

2 large eggs, separated

Kosher salt

Freshly ground black pepper

5 cups cold cooked brown rice (Baked Brown Rice, page 32)

2 teaspoons sesame oil

¼ cup soy sauce, plus more to taste

Hot sauce, for serving (optional)

This speedy vegetarian rice comes together in less than 30 minutes. Try it as a side dish with Honey-Soy Salmon Burgers (page 89) or served with egg rolls for a quick yet satisfying dinner. This dish is best made with leftover cold rice, as freshly cooked rice won't crisp up properly.

1 In a large skillet, heat 2 tablespoons of olive oil over medium-high heat. Add the onion and carrots and cook for 6 to 8 minutes, until softened. Stir in the peas and garlic and cook for 2 to 3 minutes. Transfer the mixture to a plate.

2 In a medium bowl, whisk the egg whites, season with salt and pepper, and set aside. In a large bowl, stir the egg yolks into the cold rice until combined.

3 Heat the remaining 1 tablespoon of olive oil in the skillet over medium-high heat. Add the rice mixture and stir-fry for 5 to 6 minutes, until golden brown. Make a well in the center of the skillet, then pour in the sesame oil and egg whites and stir until cooked through.

4 Add the vegetables to the skillet along with the soy sauce. Stir to combine and season to taste with salt and pepper before removing from the heat. Serve with hot sauce, if desired.

RECIPE RIFFS

Chicken Fried Rice: Add 2 cups of cubed cooked chicken to the recipe in step 4. Season with additional soy sauce to taste.

Shrimp Fried Rice: Add 1 pound of cooked small shrimp to the recipe. Season with additional soy sauce to taste.

peanut noodle salad

DAIRY-FREE · VEGAN

SERVES 4

PREP: 10 MINUTES

COOK: 10 MINUTES

8 ounces dried spaghetti

1 cup Peanut Sauce
   (page 22)

1 cup shredded carrot

½ cup chopped fresh
   cilantro

This recipe is a perfect use for my favorite Peanut Sauce (page 22). Cool and refreshing, this noodle salad can be prepared ahead of time for a quick lunch. You could also serve this dish with grilled salmon fillets for a speedy and satisfying dinner.

1 In a pot of salted boiling water, cook the spaghetti for 8 to 10 minutes, or according to the package directions. Drain and rinse well with cold water.

2 Toss the cooled pasta in a large bowl with the peanut sauce. Stir in the carrot and cilantro.

RECIPE RIFF

Peanut Noodle Salad with Salmon: Mix equal parts maple syrup and soy sauce. Brush salmon fillets with the mixture and sprinkle with red chili flakes if desired. Bake at 425°F for 10 to 12 minutes, until firm and opaque. Serve with the noodles.

IN A PINCH: Out of carrots? No worries! Chopped bell peppers and cucumbers are also great in this cold salad. Chopped peanuts also make a wonderful garnish.

nourishing grain bowls

VEGETARIAN

SERVES 4

PREP: 15 MINUTES

FOR THE TAHINI DRESSING

⅓ cup tahini

½ cup water

Juice of 1 lemon

1 teaspoon honey

2 garlic cloves, minced

½ teaspoon ground cumin

½ teaspoon kosher salt

⅛ teaspoon freshly ground black pepper

⅛ teaspoon cayenne pepper

FOR THE GRAIN BOWLS

2 cups cooked grains or pasta:

- Farro
- Rice
- Quinoa
- Pasta

2 cups cooked protein:

- Boneless skinless chicken breast
- Seasoned ground beef (warmed, if desired)
- Chickpeas or pinto beans, rinsed and drained

4 cups greens:

- Spinach
- Spring mix
- Green leaf lettuce

1 (15-ounce) can corn, drained

¼ cup fresh cilantro, chopped

Grain bowls are a tasty and healthy way to get a quick lunch or dinner on the table. The flavor combinations are endless, and most of the components can be prepped ahead of time. As you're cooking other meals, think about leftovers strategically. Try cooking extra grains and protein and store them in the refrigerator to make a grain bowl later in the week.

1 **To make the tahini dressing:** Whisk together all the tahini dressing ingredients and set aside.

2 **To make the grain bowls:** Set out 4 bowls. Place ½ cup each of grains and protein in each bowl, along with 1 cup of greens. Divide the corn among the bowls and top with fresh cilantro. Drizzle tahini dressing over each bowl and serve.

RECIPE RIFFS

Greek-Inspired Chicken Bowls: Follow the recipe as directed, using boneless skinless chicken breast as the protein. Omit the corn and cilantro and instead top the bowls with diced tomatoes, cucumber, feta cheese, and chopped parsley.

Salmon and Black Bean Bowls: Follow the recipe as directed, using 2 large baked salmon fillets as the protein. Replace the corn with 1 (15-ounce) can of black beans, rinsed and drained. Garnish with sliced scallions and red pepper flakes.

STORAGE TIP: You can prepare these grain bowls ahead of time, storing the dressing separately, for easy lunches throughout the week. The tahini dressing can be stored in the refrigerator for up to 2 weeks.

vegetable-chickpea curry

DAIRY-FREE · VEGAN

SERVES 4

PREP: 15 MINUTES

COOK: 20 MINUTES

4 tablespoons olive oil, divided

1 medium yellow onion, chopped

2 carrots, peeled and chopped

2 medium russet potatoes, peeled and chopped into bite-size pieces

3 garlic cloves, minced

2 teaspoons garam masala

2 teaspoons kosher salt

1 teaspoon ground cumin

1 teaspoon turmeric

1 teaspoon paprika

1 (14-ounce) can full-fat coconut milk

¾ cup water

2 tablespoons creamy peanut butter

2 tablespoons soy sauce

1 tablespoon brown sugar

Juice of 1 lime

2 cups frozen peas, thawed

1 (15-ounce) can chickpeas, drained and rinsed

If you've never tried making curry at home, don't be intimidated! There are a lot of ingredients, but the flavors are delicious, and it can be made in less time than it takes to get takeout. Try serving this curry over rice (such as Baked Brown Rice, page 32) with a sprinkle of cilantro.

1 In a large skillet, heat 2 tablespoons of the oil over medium heat. Add the onion and carrots and sauté for 6 to 8 minutes, until softened.

2 Meanwhile, bring a pot of salted water to a boil and cook the potatoes until tender. Drain and set aside.

3 Add the remaining 2 tablespoons of oil to the skillet along with the garlic, garam masala, salt, cumin, turmeric, and paprika. Cook over medium heat for 2 to 3 minutes to toast the spices and develop the flavors.

4 Stir in the coconut milk, water, peanut butter, soy sauce, brown sugar, and lime juice. Bring to a simmer, then taste and adjust the seasoning if desired.

5 Stir in the cooked potatoes, peas, and chickpeas. Simmer until heated through.

RECIPE RIFF

Chicken Curry: Substitute 2 boneless skinless chicken breasts, cooked and cubed, for the chickpeas and 1 chopped red bell pepper for the onion.

COOKING TIP: This is one of those recipes that requires adjusting the seasonings according to your taste. Don't be afraid to add more spices to make it your own!

spicy beef and potato tacos

DAIRY-FREE

SERVES 4 TO 6

PREP: 10 MINUTES

COOK: 20 MINUTES

1 medium russet potato, peeled and diced

1 pound 90-percent lean ground beef

3 garlic cloves, minced

2 teaspoons ground cumin

1½ teaspoons kosher salt

¼ teaspoon cayenne pepper

2 tablespoons tomato paste

½ cup water

12 (6-inch) flour or corn tortillas

Shredded cheese, lettuce, onion, sour cream, and salsa, for serving (optional)

Potatoes are an inexpensive and tasty way to stretch ground beef to feed more people. I recommend topping these tacos with a combination of shredded cheese, chopped lettuce and onion, sour cream, and Speedy Salsa (page 28). You can also use this filling mixture in Quick Quesadillas (page 37) or stuffed in enchiladas.

1 Place the potatoes in a small saucepan and cover with cold water. Bring to a boil and cook for 12 to 15 minutes, until tender. Drain and set aside.

2 While the potatoes are cooking, in a skillet, sauté the ground beef and garlic over medium-high heat for 6 to 8 minutes, until no longer pink. Drain, if desired.

3 Reduce the heat to medium, then add the cumin, salt, and cayenne pepper to the skillet. Stir to combine.

4 Add the tomato paste and cook for 2 to 3 minutes. Stir in the water and cook until heated through and mixture is thickened, about 3 minutes. Stir in the potato, then remove from the heat and adjust the seasonings as desired.

5 Warm the tortillas and top with the beef filling and your choice of toppings.

RECIPE RIFF

Pork and Potatoes with Peas: Substitute ground pork for the beef and fold in 1 cup of thawed peas after adding the tomato paste.

savory hand pies

SERVES 4

PREP: **35 MINUTES**

COOK: **25 MINUTES**

1 tablespoon olive oil

1 pound 90-percent lean
ground beef

½ yellow onion, diced

3 garlic cloves, minced

2 tablespoons tomato paste

2 teaspoons chili powder

2 teaspoons ground cumin

1 teaspoon kosher salt, plus
more for sprinkling

½ cup plus 2 tablespoons
water, divided

1 cup shredded cheddar
cheese

2 batches Perfect Piecrust
(page 30)

1 large egg

*A healthier take on traditional deep-fried empana-
das, these baked hand pies have a tender and crispy
exterior with a delicious beef filling. My whole family
loves them!*

1 In a skillet, heat the oil over medium-high heat.
Add the ground beef, onion, and garlic and sauté
for 7 to 9 minutes, until the beef is no longer pink.
Drain and return the pan to the stove.

2 Reduce the heat to medium and add the tomato
paste, chili powder, cumin, and salt. Cook for
2 minutes, then add ½ cup of the water and continue to cook until the mixture is incorporated and
thickened. Remove from the heat and stir in the
cheddar. Set aside.

3 Preheat the oven to 400°F. Line a baking sheet
with parchment paper and set aside.

4 Roll out the pie dough on a well-floured surface
until it is about ¼-inch thick. Use a 4-inch circle
cutter (or the outline of a bowl and a paring knife)
to cut out 12 circles of dough.

5 Place about 2 tablespoons of the meat mixture in
the center of each circle of dough. Fold them over
into half-moons and crimp the edges with a fork.
Transfer the pies to the prepared baking sheet.

6 Beat the egg with the remaining 2 tablespoons
of water. Brush each hand pie with the egg wash,
then sprinkle with kosher salt. Bake for 10 to
12 minutes, until golden brown.

Cherry Hand Pies: For a great dessert option, substitute cherry pie filling for the beef and sprinkle the pies with granulated sugar instead of salt.

Apple Hand Pies: Substitute apple pie filling for the beef and sprinkle with cinnamon sugar instead of salt.

STORAGE TIP: These hand pies can be prepared through step 5, then frozen. To bake from frozen, add 5 to 6 minutes to the baking time.

enchiladas with red sauce

VEGETARIAN

SERVES 4

PREP: 15 MINUTES, PLUS 10 MINUTES TO COOL

COOK: 35 MINUTES

FOR THE RED SAUCE

2 tablespoons unsalted butter, plus more for greasing the pan

1 garlic clove, minced

2 tablespoons all-purpose flour

2 cups vegetable stock

6 tablespoons tomato paste

1 teaspoon kosher salt

¾ teaspoon ground cumin

¼ teaspoon cayenne

FOR THE ENCHILADAS

2 cups cooked protein:

- 90-percent lean ground beef, cooked and drained
- Boneless skinless chicken breast, cooked and shredded
- Canned pinto beans, rinsed and drained

2 cups shredded cheese, divided:

- Cheddar
- Monterey Jack
- Pepper Jack

Kosher salt

8 (6-inch) corn tortillas

Sour cream, shredded lettuce, chopped onion, and cilantro, for serving

Homemade enchilada sauce is super simple and tastes so much better than the canned variety. Bonus: You likely already have all the ingredients in your kitchen. This flexible recipe allows you to use whatever protein you have on hand—chicken, ground beef, or beans— and the result will still be delicious!

1 Preheat the oven to 400°F. Grease a 2-quart casserole dish or an 8-by-8-inch pan with butter and set aside.

2 **To make the red sauce:** In a saucepan, melt the butter over medium heat and sauté the garlic for 2 to 3 minutes, until fragrant. Whisk in the flour and cook for 2 more minutes.

3 Add the vegetable stock, tomato paste, salt, cumin, and cayenne. Whisk until combined. Increase the heat to medium-high and cook, stirring frequently, for 2 to 3 minutes, until the mixture thickens. Set aside to cool.

4 **To make the enchiladas:** Pour ¼ cup of the red sauce into the prepared casserole dish and spread it to cover the bottom.

5 In a bowl, stir together your protein of choice, ½ cup of enchilada sauce, and ½ cup of cheese. Season the filling to taste with salt.

6 Wrap the tortillas in damp paper towels and microwave for about 30 seconds, until they are warm and pliable.

7 Place approximately ¼ cup of filling in each tortilla, then roll to seal. Place the enchiladas, seam-side down, in the dish.

8 Pour the remaining sauce over the enchiladas and sprinkle with the remaining 1½ cups of cheese.

9 Cover the dish with foil and bake for 20 minutes. Remove the foil and bake until the cheese is bubbly, about 5 more minutes.

10 Let cool for 5 to 10 minutes before serving with sour cream, shredded lettuce, chopped onion, and cilantro.

STORAGE TIP: You can prepare this recipe ahead of time through step 8, then cover the pan and refrigerate. When you're ready to finish the enchiladas, add 10 minutes to the baking time. If you're using a glass dish, be sure not to transfer it directly from the refrigerator to the oven, which can cause it to break. Instead, let it come to room temperature before baking.

homestyle macaroni goulash

DAIRY-FREE

2 tablespoons olive oil

1 pound 90-percent lean ground beef

1 small onion, diced

2 garlic cloves, minced

2 cups water

1 (15-ounce) can crushed tomatoes

1 (15-ounce) can diced tomatoes, undrained

1 tablespoon Italian seasoning

1 tablespoon soy sauce

2 teaspoons granulated sugar

1 teaspoon kosher salt

½ teaspoon freshly ground black pepper

1 cup dried macaroni

Goulash is one of those meals that transports me back to my childhood. Soy sauce may seem like an odd ingredient here, but it adds a depth of flavor and balances out the sweetness of the tomatoes. A hearty and crowd-pleasing dish, this dinner is best served with a green salad and some garlic Focaccia (page 118) on the side.

1 In a soup pot or Dutch oven, heat the oil over medium-high heat. Add the ground beef, onion, and garlic and sauté for 8 to 10 minutes, or until cooked through. Drain, if desired.

2 Add the water, crushed tomatoes, diced tomatoes, Italian seasoning, soy sauce, sugar, salt, and pepper. Cover and simmer over medium-low heat for 15 to 20 minutes.

3 Stir in the macaroni and continue to simmer for about 20 minutes, or until the pasta is tender, adding more water if necessary to keep the goulash from sticking to the sides of the pot.

4 Remove from the heat and let sit for 10 to 15 minutes to thicken before serving.

IN A PINCH: No ground beef on hand? Try using Italian sausage or ground turkey instead. Also, any short pasta can be substituted for the macaroni.

penne al forno

SERVES 6 TO 8

PREP: 10 MINUTES, PLUS
10 MINUTES TO STAND

COOK: 40 MINUTES

Butter or oil, for greasing
the casserole dish

1 pound dried penne pasta

2 cups Alfredo
Sauce (page 23)

3 cups Marinara Sauce
(page 24)

2 cups shredded mozzarella
cheese

The Italian phrase al forno literally translates to "baked." This hearty pasta dish is finished in the oven for a comforting and fuss-free meal. Try serving it with Garlic Cheese Sticks (page 121) and a green salad.

1 Heat the oven to 350°F. Grease a 9-by-13-inch casserole dish with butter or oil and set aside.

2 Bring a large pot of salted water to a rapid boil and add the penne. Cook for 8 to 9 minutes, until almost tender, or according to package directions. Drain.

3 Stir the Alfredo sauce into the cooked pasta.

4 Place half of the pasta in the casserole dish. Top with 1½ cups of the marinara sauce, then 1 cup of the mozzarella. Top with the remaining half of the pasta, then layer on the remaining 1½ cups of marinara and remaining 1 cup of mozzarella.

5 Bake until the edges are golden and bubbly, about 30 minutes. Allow to stand for 10 minutes before serving.

COOKING TIP: Do not overcook the penne in step 2 since the pasta will continue to cook in the oven.

IN A PINCH: If you're short on time, used jarred sauces in lieu of homemade.

RECIPE RIFFS

Sausage and Pepper Penne al Forno: Sauté 1 pound of Italian sausage with 1 sliced bell pepper until cooked through. Drain and add to the marinara sauce before assembling the dish.

Chicken and Pepper Penne al Forno: Sauté 1 pound of cubed boneless skinless chicken breast with 1 sliced bell pepper until cooked through, then season with salt and pepper. Add the chicken and pepper to the marinara sauce before assembling the dish.

cheesy chicken and broccoli bake

Butter or oil, for greasing the casserole dish

2 boneless skinless chicken breasts

Kosher salt

Freshly ground black pepper

2 tablespoons olive oil

1 (12-ounce) bag frozen broccoli florets

1 (10-ounce) can condensed cream of chicken soup

1 cup sour cream

⅓ cup milk

Juice of 1 lemon

2 teaspoons Dijon mustard

2½ cups cooked brown rice (Baked Brown Rice, page 32)

2½ cups shredded cheddar cheese, divided

This rich, creamy casserole is the ultimate comfort meal. The addition of lemon juice and Dijon mustard might seem unconventional, but they balance out the flavors perfectly. Serve with a fresh salad and dinner is done!

1 Preheat the oven to 375°F. Grease a 2-quart casserole dish with butter or oil and set aside.

2 Season the chicken breasts on both sides with salt and pepper. In a nonstick skillet, heat the oil over medium-high heat and sauté the chicken for 4 to 5 minutes on each side, or until cooked through. Remove from the pan, cover with foil, and set aside.

3 Cook the broccoli according to the package directions.

4 In a large bowl, whisk together the soup, sour cream, milk, lemon juice, and mustard until well combined. Fold in the rice, cooked broccoli, and 2 cups of the cheddar.

5 Cut the chicken breasts into bite-size cubes, then stir them into the rice mixture. Pour the mixture into the prepared casserole dish and top with the remaining ½ cup of cheddar.

6 Bake for 30 to 35 minutes, until the cheese is bubbly and the casserole is heated through.

RECIPE RIFFS

Low-Carb Broccoli-Chicken Bake: Substitute cooked cauliflower rice for the brown rice.

Beef and Mushroom Casserole: Omit the chicken and broccoli. Instead, sauté 1 pound of lean ground beef and 2 cups of sliced mushrooms until the beef is cooked through. Drain thoroughly and season with salt and pepper. Add the beef and mushrooms to the rice mixture and bake as directed.

IN A PINCH: A variety of vegetables can be substituted for the broccoli. Green beans or sautéed mushrooms would be a welcome addition!

spaghetti pizza with pepperoni

SERVES 4 TO 6

PREP: 15 MINUTES, PLUS
5 MINUTES TO STAND

COOK: 50 MINUTES

Butter or oil, for greasing
the casserole dish

8 ounces dried spaghetti

⅓ cup milk

⅓ cup grated Parmesan
cheese

1 large egg

2 garlic cloves, minced

½ teaspoon kosher salt

2 cups shredded mozzarella
cheese, divided

3 cups Marinara Sauce
(page 24)

1 teaspoon Italian seasoning

4 ounces sliced pepperoni

Another recipe from my childhood, this unique casserole incorporates all the flavors of a classic pizza but uses cooked spaghetti for the crust! This dish is a definite crowd-pleaser and is easy to prepare in advance: Store the casserole in the refrigerator after assembling the layers, then all you need to do is bake it on the night you want to serve it. If you like, sub in store-bought marinara for the homemade stuff.

1 Preheat the oven to 425°F. Grease a 9-by-13-inch casserole dish with butter or oil and set aside.

2 Bring a pot of salted water to boil and add the spaghetti. Cook for 8 to 10 minutes, until almost tender, or according to package directions. Drain and rinse with cool water. Set aside.

3 In a large bowl, whisk together the milk, Parmesan, egg, garlic, salt, and ¼ cup of the mozzarella cheese. Add the cooked spaghetti and toss to combine.

4 Pour the spaghetti mixture into the prepared casserole dish. Bake for 15 minutes, then remove it from the oven.

5 Reduce the oven temperature to 350°F. Spread the marinara sauce on top of the casserole. Then top with the remaining 1¾ cups of mozzarella and sprinkle with the Italian seasoning. Place the pepperoni over the cheese in a single layer.

6 Bake for 25 more minutes, or until hot and bubbly. Let stand for 5 minutes before cutting into pieces and serving.

RECIPE RIFF

Supreme Spaghetti Pizza: Stir cooked and crumbled Italian sausage into the marinara sauce before assembling. Add toppings such as onions, peppers, or olives along with the pepperoni.

IN A PINCH: Have a jar of store-bought marinara? This is a great use for it!

Minestrone Soup, page 70

legumes and vegetables

The stars of this chapter are protein-rich legumes in dishes like Chickpea and Carrot Salad and Cajun-Inspired Beans and Rice. You'll also find delicious soup recipes using staple vegetables, including Broccoli-Cheddar Soup and Curried Carrot Soup. For a delicious appetizer, try the Corn and Bean Salad or Classic Hummus. I've also included satisfying main dishes, like Chilaquiles and my favorite, the Cheesy Potato Bake.

classic hummus

DAIRY-FREE · GLUTEN-FREE · VEGAN

YIELD: 2 CUPS

PREP: 10 MINUTES,

PLUS 2 HOURS TO CHILL

1 (15-ounce) can chickpeas, drained and rinsed

Juice of 1 lemon

¼ cup tahini

2 tablespoons olive oil

2 garlic cloves, minced

½ teaspoon kosher salt

¼ teaspoon ground cumin

⅛ teaspoon cayenne pepper

⅓ cup cold water

Have you ever made hummus at home? Once you try it, you'll never go back to the packaged variety. Homemade hummus is so creamy and delicious, and it's very easy to customize with your favorite herbs and seasonings.

1 Pulse the chickpeas and lemon juice in a food processor until the mixture resembles coarse sand. Add the tahini, oil, garlic, salt, cumin, and cayenne and process until smooth.

2 With the food processor running, slowly stream in the cold water. Allow the mixture to process for 3 to 4 minutes, until it is very smooth and creamy. Taste and adjust the seasonings.

3 Transfer the hummus to an airtight container and refrigerate for at least 2 hours before serving.

RECIPE RIFFS

Roasted Red Pepper Hummus: For a different flavor profile, add ¼ cup of roasted red peppers and ½ teaspoon of paprika with the tahini.

Jalapeno-Cilantro Hummus: Add 1 seeded and chopped jalapeño pepper and ½ cup of fresh cilantro to the food processor with the tahini.

COOKING TIP: Hummus is great served with raw vegetables such as carrots, peppers, and cucumber. It's also delicious with pita bread, crackers, or spread in a Mediterranean-inspired wrap!

STORAGE TIP: Hummus will keep in the refrigerator for 5 to 7 days.

green salad with apples and candied walnuts

DAIRY-FREE · GLUTEN-FREE · VEGETARIAN

SERVES 4

PREP: 10 MINUTES

COOK: 15 MINUTES

FOR THE WALNUTS

2 cups walnuts

2 tablespoons granulated sugar

2 tablespoons honey

1 tablespoon olive oil

¼ teaspoon kosher salt

¼ teaspoon ground cinnamon

Pinch cayenne pepper

FOR THE SALAD

1 large head green leaf lettuce, chopped

2 apples, cored and thinly sliced

⅓ cup dried cranberries

Simple Vinaigrette (page 18), for serving

This salad is full of crunch and fantastic flavors. Serve it as a side dish with dinner or add protein, such as chicken or salmon, for a hearty meal. I promise, the extra step of candying the walnuts is absolutely worth it.

1 **To make the walnuts:** Preheat the oven to 350°F. Line a baking sheet with parchment paper and set aside.

2 In a small bowl, combine the walnuts, sugar, honey, oil, salt, cinnamon, and cayenne. Stir well to combine.

3 Pour the walnuts onto the prepared baking sheet and bake for 12 to 15 minutes. Remove from the oven and allow to cool.

4 **To make the salad:** Assemble the salads by dividing the lettuce, apples, and cranberries among 4 bowls. Alternatively, layer the ingredients in a large serving bowl. Top with the cooled walnuts and serve with vinaigrette.

RECIPE RIFF

Steak and Blue Cheese Salad: Top the salads with sliced steak and blue cheese before dressing with the vinaigrette.

COOKING TIP: Cooling the candied walnuts is an important step, as it allows the glaze to crisp up.

bean burritos

VEGETARIAN

SERVES 4

PREP: **10 MINUTES**

COOK: **15 MINUTES**

2 tablespoons olive oil

2 garlic cloves, minced

2 (15-ounce) cans pinto beans, drained with liquid reserved

Juice of 1 lime

1 teaspoon kosher salt

½ teaspoon ground cumin

4 (10- to 12-inch) flour tortillas

2 cups shredded cheddar cheese

Sour cream, salsa, and cilantro, for serving (optional)

COOKING TIP: Use as much of the bean liquid as you like to thin the beans to your desired texture. Don't skip the final step, as crisping the burritos in a dry pan helps seal the filling in and add crunch to the exterior.

REINVENT IT: Have extra beans left over? Use them the next morning in a breakfast tostada or egg burrito.

These meatless burritos are super quick to put together and are perfect for busy weeknights. Homemade refried beans are a cinch to make with canned pinto beans and taste so fresh. Feel free to customize this recipe with your favorite burrito fixings, like guacamole, Speedy Salsa (page 28), chopped cilantro, or sliced jalapenos.

1 In a large skillet, heat the oil over medium heat. Add the garlic and sauté for a minute or two, until fragrant.

2 Add the drained beans to the pan and use a potato masher to mash most of the beans. Stir in ¼ cup of the bean liquid (or more if desired, to thin), the lime juice, salt, and cumin. Cook, stirring often, over medium heat until heated through. Remove from the heat and adjust the seasoning to taste.

3 Divide the beans evenly among the tortillas. Sprinkle with the cheese. If desired, top with sour cream, salsa, or cilantro.

4 Roll up the burritos with the ends tucked in. In a dry skillet, place the burritos seam-side down and cook over medium heat until lightly browned, about 2 to 3 minutes. Flip to crisp up the other side before serving, another 2 to 3 minutes.

RECIPE RIFF

Bean and Chorizo Burritos: Cook and drain 1 pound of chorizo sausage. Add to the burritos in step 3.

curried carrot soup

DAIRY-FREE · GLUTEN-FREE · VEGAN

SERVES 4

PREP: 10 MINUTES

COOK: 20 MINUTES

2 tablespoons olive oil

5 or 6 large carrots, peeled and chopped

1 medium yellow onion, chopped

3 garlic cloves, minced

4 cups vegetable stock

2 teaspoons garam masala

1 teaspoon kosher salt

1 teaspoon ground cumin

1 teaspoon turmeric

1 teaspoon paprika

¼ teaspoon freshly ground black pepper

1 (15-ounce) can full-fat coconut milk

Juice of 1 lime

This soup is packed with vegetables and makes a healthy, flavorful meal served with crusty bread or croutons or as a satisfying side to your dinner. Try it with Chickpea and Carrot Salad (page 62) or a grilled cheese sandwich.

1   In a large soup pot, heat the oil over medium-high heat. Add the carrots and onion and sauté for 5 to 6 minutes, until softened. Add the garlic and cook about 2 minutes, until fragrant.

2   Add the stock, garam masala, salt, cumin, turmeric, paprika, and pepper. Bring to a boil, then reduce the heat to medium and simmer for 8 to 10 minutes, until the vegetables are very tender.

3   Remove the pot from the heat and use an immersion blender to puree the soup. Alternatively, transfer the soup to a blender in batches and puree (careful, it's hot!) before returning it to the pot.

4   Over medium heat, stir in the coconut milk. Cook until the soup is hot, then stir in the lime juice. Taste and adjust the seasoning.

STORAGE TIP: This soup can be stored in the refrigerator for 3 to 5 days or frozen for up to 3 months. Reheat slowly and whisk to combine.

corn and bean salad

DAIRY-FREE · GLUTEN-FREE · VEGAN

SERVES 6 TO 8

PREP: 10 MINUTES,
PLUS 2 HOURS TO CHILL

6 tablespoons rice wine
vinegar

6 tablespoons olive oil

2 garlic cloves, minced

2 teaspoons ground cumin

1 teaspoon Italian seasoning

½ teaspoon kosher salt

¼ teaspoon freshly ground
black pepper

1 (15-ounce) can pinto
beans, rinsed and drained

1 (15-ounce) can corn,
drained

1 (15-ounce) can diced
tomatoes, drained

1 small onion, diced

½ cup chopped fresh
cilantro

This tasty bean salad can be served on its own, but I love it with tortilla chips as a quick lunch or party appetizer. It also pairs well with tacos and quesadillas. This dish tastes even better after resting in the refrigerator, so make it ahead of time for the best results.

1   In a large bowl, whisk together the vinegar, oil, garlic, cumin, Italian seasoning, salt, and pepper until well combined.

2   Add the beans, corn, tomatoes, onion, and cilantro and stir well. Refrigerate for at least 2 hours before serving. Adjust the seasonings to taste.

broccoli-cheddar soup

VEGETARIAN

SERVES 4

PREP: 10 MINUTES

COOK: 25 MINUTES

3 tablespoons unsalted butter

1 medium onion, diced

2 cups shredded carrot

2 garlic cloves, minced

⅓ cup all-purpose flour

½ teaspoon kosher salt

¼ teaspoon freshly ground black pepper

⅛ teaspoon cayenne pepper

3 cups vegetable stock

1 pound frozen broccoli florets

2 cups milk

2 cups shredded cheddar cheese

This flavorful soup is one you'll crave on chilly fall and winter evenings. Serve this soup with a bit of extra shredded cheese and a side of Focaccia (page 118) or crackers. You can also get fancy and serve it in bread bowls!

1 In a large soup pot, melt the butter over medium heat. Add the onion, carrots, and garlic and sauté for about 8 minutes, until tender.

2 Stir in the flour, salt, pepper, and cayenne. Cook for 2 minutes.

3 Stir in the vegetable stock and broccoli and bring to a boil. Reduce the heat to medium and simmer for about 10 minutes, until the broccoli is tender.

4 Reduce the heat to medium-low and stir in the milk and cheddar. Heat until the cheese is melted. Adjust the seasoning to taste before serving.

RECIPE RIFFS

Chicken, Broccoli, and Cheddar Soup: Add 2 cups of cubed cooked chicken before step 4.

Cauliflower-Cheddar Soup: Omit the carrots and substitute 1 pound of frozen or fresh cauliflower for the broccoli. Serve with cooked and crumbled bacon, if desired.

STORAGE TIP: Leftovers can be stored in the refrigerator for 4 days and reheated on the stovetop or in the microwave. Unfortunately, this soup does not freeze well.

chickpea and carrot salad

DAIRY-FREE · GLUTEN-FREE · VEGETARIAN

SERVES 4

PREP: 15 MINUTES

FOR THE DRESSING

2 garlic cloves, minced

¼ cup lemon juice

3 tablespoons olive oil

2 tablespoons honey

1 teaspoon ground cumin

1 teaspoon garam masala

½ teaspoon kosher salt

¼ teaspoon cayenne
  pepper

FOR THE SALAD

1 (15-ounce) can chickpeas,
  rinsed and drained

2 cups shredded carrot

½ cup chopped cilantro

½ cup dried cranberries

½ cup chopped walnuts,
  toasted

2 tablespoons onion, finely
  minced

This bright and fresh salad is the perfect accompaniment to dinner and also makes a healthy lunch. Since the ingredients in this salad are so hearty, it holds up well in the refrigerator. To make this easy recipe even quicker, try using a food processor to shred the carrots.

1 **To make the dressing:** In a small bowl, whisk together all the dressing ingredients, or put them in a glass jar and shake until combined.

2 **To make the salad:** In a large bowl, combine the chickpeas, carrots, cilantro, cranberries, walnuts, and onion. Note: To toast raw walnuts, place them in a dry skillet over medium heat and cook until fragrant. Be careful, as they burn quickly.

3 Pour the dressing over the salad ingredients and stir to combine. Adjust the seasoning to taste before serving or storing for later.

RECIPE RIFF

Greek-Inspired Chickpea Salad: Omit the cilantro, cranberries, and walnuts. Instead, use ½ cup of chopped flat-leaf parsley, 1 cup of chopped cucumber, and 1 cup of halved cherry tomatoes. Make the dressing as directed, omitting the cumin and garam masala and adding 1 teaspoon of Italian seasoning.

STORAGE TIP: This salad can be made and stored in the refrigerator for up to 4 days.

IN A PINCH: Substitute parsley for cilantro or almonds for walnuts. White beans are also a great substitute for chickpeas.

cajun-inspired beans and rice

DAIRY-FREE · GLUTEN-FREE

SERVES 4

PREP: 10 MINUTES

COOK: 35 MINUTES

2 tablespoons olive oil

1 medium onion, chopped

4 garlic cloves, minced

12 ounces fully cooked beef smoked sausage, sliced

2 (15-ounce) cans pinto beans, drained

2 cups vegetable stock

1½ teaspoons Italian seasoning

1 teaspoon paprika

1 teaspoon kosher salt

½ teaspoon cayenne pepper

½ teaspoon freshly ground black pepper

Cooked rice, for serving

Traditionally, this dish is made with dark-red kidney beans, though nearly any type of bean will work in this recipe. Whatever type you choose, don't skip the smoked sausage, which brings a rich, salty flavor to the beans. Cut back on the cayenne if you don't care for spicy foods.

1 In a large skillet, heat the oil over medium-high heat. Add the onion and cook for 4 to 5 minutes. Stir in the garlic and sliced sausage and cook for about 10 more minutes, until the sausage is browned and the onions are cooked through.

2 Stir in the beans, stock, Italian seasoning, paprika, salt, cayenne, and pepper. Bring to a boil, then reduce the heat to medium. Simmer partially covered for 20 minutes, until slightly thickened.

3 Serve hot over rice.

> **COOKING TIP:** If you have green peppers and celery on hand, they make welcome additions to this dish. You can also use any type of smoked sausage that you'd like, including turkey or andouille.

chilaquiles

VEGETARIAN

SERVES 4

PREP: 15 MINUTES

COOK: 15 MINUTES

FOR THE CHIPS

8 (6-inch) corn tortillas

½ cup olive oil

Kosher salt

FOR THE CHILAQUILES

2 (14-ounce) cans diced
tomatoes, drained

2 cups vegetable stock

1 medium yellow onion,
diced

4 garlic cloves, minced

1 teaspoon kosher salt

½ teaspoon cayenne
pepper

1 tablespoon olive oil, plus
more for greasing the
skillet

4 large eggs

Kosher salt

Freshly ground black
pepper

Sour cream and cilantro, for
serving (optional)

Chilaquiles are a traditional Mexican dish of corn tortilla chips simmered in a savory tomato broth. They are absolutely amazing, and my spin on the dish has become one of my favorite breakfasts! Try serving them with a fried egg for extra protein, or simply top them with sour cream and cilantro.

1 **To make the chips:** Cut each tortilla into 6 triangular wedges. In a skillet, heat the olive oil over medium-high heat until it is shimmering. Fry the tortillas in batches until golden brown, 2 to 3 minutes on each side. Transfer to a plate lined with a paper towel and sprinkle lightly with salt while hot. Set aside.

2 **To make the chilaquiles:** In a blender or food processor, add the tomatoes, stock, onion, garlic, salt, and cayenne and blend until smooth.

3 In a large skillet, heat the oil over medium-high heat. Add the tomato mixture and cook for 5 to 10 minutes, until slightly thickened. Taste and adjust the seasonings as desired.

4 Add the tortilla chips to the skillet and turn to coat. Cook over medium heat for 2 to 3 minutes, then remove from the heat.

5 Fry the eggs in a small greased skillet, then season with salt and pepper.

6 Divide the chilaquiles among 4 plates and top each plate with an egg. Serve with sour cream and cilantro, if desired.

RECIPE RIFF

Loaded Chilaquiles: Season a sliced avocado with salt, pepper, and lime juice. Top the finished chilaquiles with the avocado along with shredded Monterey Jack cheese.

STORAGE TIP: This dish is best served immediately; the chips will continue to soak up liquid and become soggy.

breakfast quesadillas

VEGETARIAN

SERVES 4

PREP: 15 MINUTES

COOK: 15 MINUTES

6 large eggs

¼ cup milk

1 teaspoon kosher salt

1 tablespoon olive oil

8 (8-inch) flour tortillas

2 tablespoons unsalted butter, melted

1 cup cooked protein:

- Cooked ham, diced
- Cooked and crumbled bacon
- Cooked and crumbled breakfast sausage
- Pinto beans, drained and rinsed

1 cup shredded cheese:

- Cheddar
- Monterey Jack
- Pepper Jack

1 cup sautéed vegetables:

- Onions
- Peppers
- Mushrooms

Have you ever heard of a breakfast quesadilla? You're in for a treat! These are totally customizable and totally delicious. Try serving them with Speedy Salsa (page 28) and sour cream on the side.

1 In a large bowl, whisk together the eggs, milk, and salt. In a nonstick skillet, heat the oil over medium heat, then pour in the egg mixture. Slowly cook for 4 to 5 minutes, stirring until the eggs are cooked through. Remove the skillet from the heat.

2 Brush one side of each tortilla with the melted butter. In a second nonstick skillet, place a tortilla buttered-side down. Add ¼ cup of protein, ¼ cup of cheese, ¼ cup of vegetables, and one-quarter of the egg mixture. Place another tortilla on top, buttered-side up.

3 Cook the quesadilla over medium heat until brown and crispy. Flip the quesadilla and continue cooking until the other side is also browned. Repeat with the remaining tortillas and fillings.

4 Cut each tortilla into quarters and serve.

COOKING TIP: Keep the prepared quesadillas warm in an oven preheated to 250°F.

bacon and potato hash with eggs

GLUTEN-FREE

SERVES 4

PREP: 10 MINUTES

COOK: 20 MINUTES

2 tablespoons unsalted butter

1 tablespoon olive oil

1 (28-ounce) bag frozen cubed potatoes

½ medium yellow onion, diced

3 teaspoons kosher salt, divided

½ teaspoon freshly ground black pepper

12 ounces bacon

6 large eggs

¼ cup milk

1 cup shredded cheddar cheese

Looking for a quick and simple breakfast? With crispy potatoes, salty bacon, and creamy eggs, this delicious hash has something for everyone. Try not to eat the whole pan!

1 In a large skillet, heat the butter and oil over medium-high heat. Add the potatoes, onion, 2 teaspoons of salt, and pepper. Cook for 10 to 12 minutes, until the potatoes are light brown and crispy.

2 While the potatoes are cooking, in a second skillet, crisp the bacon over medium-high heat. Transfer to a plate lined with paper towels, then cut it into bite-size pieces. Discard the bacon grease and wipe out the skillet.

3 In a bowl, whisk together the eggs, milk, and remaining 1 teaspoon of salt. Pour the egg mixture into the skillet and cook over medium heat until the eggs are cooked through. Remove from the heat.

4 Stir the bacon into the potatoes, then top with the cheese. Divide the potatoes and eggs among 4 plates and serve.

RECIPE RIFFS

Veggie Potato Hash with Eggs: Sauté sliced bell peppers, mushrooms, and jalapeños in a skillet with olive oil instead of bacon. Continue with the recipe as directed.

Spicy Bacon and Potato Hash with Eggs: Add 1 chopped jalapeno to the recipe in step 1 (remove the seeds for less spice). Add 1 teaspoon of hot sauce to the eggs before cooking. Serve with Speedy Salsa (page 28).

veggie burgers

DAIRY-FREE · VEGETARIAN

1 (15-ounce) can pinto
  beans, drained and rinsed

½ cup panko bread crumbs

⅓ cup walnuts

1 large egg

2 garlic cloves, minced

1 teaspoon kosher salt

1 teaspoon ground cumin

1 teaspoon hot sauce

¼ teaspoon freshly ground
  black pepper

2 tablespoons olive oil

COOKING TIP: Placing
the patties between
sheets of wax paper
makes them easier to
form. The patties can
be fragile, so take care
when turning them in
the skillet.

STORAGE TIP: These
burgers can be formed
into patties and frozen
for up to 3 months.
Thaw in the refrigerator
before cooking.

*Even meat eaters will love these hearty veggie burgers
packed with protein! Serve them on toasted buns with
all the classic toppings as a great option for Meatless
Mondays. My favorites are lettuce, tomatoes, pickles,
cheese, and an array of condiments.*

1 In a food processor, pulse the beans until
   coarsely chopped.

2 Add the bread crumbs, walnuts, egg, garlic, salt,
   cumin, hot sauce, and pepper. Process the mixture
   until well combined.

3 Transfer the mixture to a bowl and refrigerate for at
   least 20 minutes, or up to 24 hours.

4 When ready to cook, in a nonstick skillet, heat
   the oil over medium-high heat. Form the mixture into 4 patties and cook the burgers for 4 to
   5 minutes on each side, until golden brown and
   heated through.

RECIPE RIFFS

Vegan Burgers: Replace the egg with a flax "egg": Mix
1 tablespoon of ground flaxseed with 2 tablespoons
of water and allow the mixture to thicken for 10 to
15 minutes before using.

Black Bean Burgers: Substitute black beans for the
pinto beans. Add ½ cup of fresh cilantro to the food processor in step 2 and prepare as directed.

cheesy potato bake

SERVES 6 TO 8

PREP: 10 MINUTES, PLUS
10 MINUTES TO COOL

COOK: 45 MINUTES

Butter or oil, for greasing
the casserole dish

1 (10-ounce) can condensed
cream of chicken soup

1 cup sour cream

½ cup milk

4 tablespoons unsalted
butter, melted

1 teaspoon kosher salt

¼ teaspoon freshly ground
black pepper

1 (26-ounce) bag frozen
shredded potatoes,
thawed

¼ cup finely diced onion

2 cups shredded cheddar
cheese

I've been making this cheesy baked dish for over 15 years, and it never disappoints. It makes a wonderful side dish for dinner or to take to a family gathering. Everyone always loves it and goes back for seconds!

1 Preheat the oven to 375°F. Grease a 9-by-13-inch casserole dish with butter or oil and set aside.

2 In a large bowl, whisk together the soup, sour cream, milk, butter, salt, and pepper until well combined.

3 Stir in the potatoes, onion, and 1¾ cups of the cheddar. Spread the mixture into the casserole dish, then top with the remaining ¼ cup of cheddar.

4 Bake for 45 minutes, or until the edges are brown and the casserole is bubbly. Allow to cool for 10 minutes before serving.

RECIPE RIFFS

Ham and Potato Casserole: For a complete meal, add 1 cup of cooked diced ham to the casserole. Top with crushed potato chips or cornflakes before baking.

Beef and Potato Casserole: Sauté ¾ pound of ground beef until cooked through, then drain well and season with salt and pepper. Add the cooked beef to the casserole before baking. Garnish with sliced scallions before serving.

STORAGE TIP: This casserole will keep for up to 5 days in the refrigerator and can be reheated easily in the microwave. Try the leftovers heated up for breakfast in the morning with a side of eggs and bacon!

minestrone soup

VEGETARIAN

SERVES 6 TO 8

PREP: 15 MINUTES

COOK: 30 MINUTES

2 tablespoons olive oil

1 medium onion, diced

3 carrots, peeled and diced

6 garlic cloves, minced

8 cups stock:

- Chicken
- Vegetable
- Beef

2 cups frozen vegetables:

- Green beans
- Peas
- Mixed vegetables

1 (28-ounce) can crushed tomatoes

1 (15-ounce) can beans, drained and rinsed:

- Red kidney beans
- Chickpeas
- Cannellini beans

1 (14-ounce) can diced tomatoes, undrained

1 tablespoon Italian seasoning

1 tablespoon kosher salt

1 teaspoon freshly ground black pepper

1 cup dried pasta:

- Macaroni
- Ditalini
- Orzo

½ cup grated Parmesan cheese

Traditionally, minestrone is an Italian soup made with vegetables, beans, pasta, and broth. This version is very flexible and can be created with a variety of different ingredients you might have on hand. Warm and comforting, this dish is perfect served with a side of grilled cheese or a crisp green salad.

1 In a large soup pot, heat the oil over medium-high heat. Add the onion and carrots and sauté for about 8 minutes, until tender. Add the garlic and cook until fragrant.

2 Stir in the stock, frozen vegetables, crushed tomatoes, beans, diced tomatoes, Italian seasoning, salt, and pepper. Bring to a boil and simmer for 10 minutes.

3 Stir in the pasta and boil for about 10 minutes, until the noodles are tender. Stir in the Parmesan and adjust the seasoning as desired.

RECIPE RIFFS

Pesto Minestrone with Croutons: For a bright pop of flavor, stir in a few tablespoons of basil pesto at the end. Serve with homemade or store-bought croutons.

Spicy Sausage Minestrone: Stir 1 pound of cooked and crumbled spicy Italian sausage and 1 teaspoon of red pepper flakes into the soup along with the vegetables.

STORAGE TIP: This soup makes great leftovers, though the pasta in the soup will expand as it sits. Add a bit more stock when reheating, if desired.

Salmon Niçoise Salad, page 74

canned and frozen seafood

The recipes in this chapter showcase the endless versatility of seafood. You'll find some unexpected dishes, like Crab Quiche and Seafood Enchiladas, as well as more traditional ones, like Tuna Noodle Casserole and Spicy Shrimp and Cheddar Grits. If you're like me and live in an area where fresh seafood is not readily available, don't feel like you can't use it in your cooking! Frozen seafood is just as delicious, and canned seafood is a budget-friendly way to add flavor and protein to your recipes.

salmon niçoise salad

DAIRY-FREE · GLUTEN-FREE

SERVES 4

PREP: 20 MINUTES

COOK: 15 MINUTES

1 pound salmon fillets

4 tablespoons olive oil, divided

Juice and zest of 2 lemons, divided

1 teaspoon dried dill

Kosher salt

Freshly ground black pepper

2 russet potatoes, peeled and cubed

2 tablespoons capers, drained

6 to 8 cups chopped green leaf lettuce

6 large hard-boiled eggs, sliced

1 cup frozen peas, thawed

Simple Vinaigrette (page 18), for serving

Niçoise salad is a French dish that is similar to the American Cobb salad. Traditionally it includes tuna, green beans, potatoes, and hard-boiled eggs. I've made a few modifications better suited to pantry cooking, but feel free to add any fresh vegetables you have in the refrigerator.

1 Preheat the oven to 400°F. Line a baking sheet with foil.

2 Place the salmon fillets on the baking sheet. Drizzle 2 tablespoons of oil over the fish, then season with the juice and zest of 1 lemon, dill, salt, and pepper.

3 Bake the salmon for 10 to 12 minutes, or until cooked through. Set aside.

4 While the salmon is baking, bring a saucepan of salted water to a boil and cook the potatoes for 10 to 15 minutes, until tender.

5 Drain the potatoes and transfer to a small bowl. Toss the potatoes with the remaining 2 tablespoons of oil, juice and zest of 1 lemon, and the capers. Season with salt and pepper.

6 In large salad bowls or plates, arrange the lettuce, salmon fillets, potatoes, eggs, and peas. Drizzle with vinaigrette and serve.

COOKING TIP: The following ingredients make great additions to this salad: blanched green beans, olives, sliced cucumber, fresh tomatoes, and chopped fresh parsley.

STORAGE TIP: The vinaigrette, salmon, eggs, and potatoes can be made ahead of time and stored in the refrigerator. Assemble the salad right before eating for a speedy meal.

crab dip with toast points

SERVES 4 TO 6

PREP: 10 MINUTES

COOK: 30 MINUTES

Butter or oil, for greasing the pie plate

1 (8-ounce) package cream cheese, at room temperature

½ cup mayonnaise

1 tablespoon Dijon mustard

1 teaspoon paprika

½ teaspoon dried dill

½ teaspoon kosher salt, plus more for sprinkling

¼ teaspoon freshly ground black pepper

¼ teaspoon cayenne pepper

2 (6-ounce) cans lump crabmeat, drained

½ cup shredded cheddar cheese

8 slices hearty gluten-free white bread, cut into triangles

3 tablespoons unsalted butter

> **COOKING TIP:** Traditionally this dip would be served as an appetizer, but it would also make an excellent light dinner when served with a salad.

This recipe is an innovative way to incorporate seafood into an appetizer. The toast points are worth the extra effort, but you can substitute crackers if you're short on time. Either way, be sure to choose gluten-free dipping options if you're cooking for anyone with a gluten sensitivity.

1 Preheat the oven to 350°F. Grease a 9-inch pie plate or 8-by-8-inch dish with butter or oil.

2 In a large bowl, combine the cream cheese, mayonnaise, mustard, paprika, dill, salt, pepper, and cayenne using an electric mixer or a heavy spoon.

3 Gently stir in the crabmeat. Place the mixture in the prepared pie plate or dish and sprinkle the cheddar on top. Bake for 30 minutes, uncovered, until the dip is bubbly and brown around the edges.

4 While the dip bakes, prepare the toast points. Cut the crusts off the bread, then cut each slice into 4 triangular pieces.

5 In a nonstick skillet, melt 1½ tablespoons of butter over medium heat. Place half of the bread in the skillet and cook until it is light brown on both sides. Transfer to a plate and sprinkle with salt. Continue with the remaining bread and 1½ tablespoons of butter.

6 Serve the dip warm with the toast points.

RECIPE RIFF

Spicy Crab Dip: Stir in 1 finely chopped jalapeño before baking. Alternatively, 1 tablespoon of diced chipotle in adobo sauce would work as well.

crab and corn chowder

SERVES 4 TO 6

PREP: 10 MINUTES

COOK: 40 MINUTES

8 ounces bacon, diced

1 medium yellow onion, diced

2 garlic cloves, minced

3 cups vegetable stock

2 medium russet potatoes, peeled and cut into bite-size pieces

1 (15-ounce) can corn, undrained

1 teaspoon paprika

1 teaspoon kosher salt

¼ teaspoon freshly ground black pepper

1 (6-ounce) can lump crabmeat, drained

3 cups milk

⅓ cup all-purpose flour

This comforting soup comes together quickly and is best served with a side of hot buttermilk biscuits or crusty bread for dipping. It can feed up to six—but be warned, you'll definitely want seconds!

1 In a large soup pot, sauté the bacon over medium heat until crisp. Remove the bacon with a slotted spoon to a plate lined with paper towels, reserving the bacon fat in the pot.

2 Add the onion to the pot and sauté over medium-high heat for 5 to 6 minutes, until softened. Add the garlic and cook until fragrant. Stir in the vegetable stock, potatoes, corn, paprika, salt, and pepper.

3 Bring to a boil and simmer for about 15 minutes, or until the potatoes are tender. Stir in the crabmeat.

4 In a medium bowl, whisk together the milk and flour until no lumps remain. Turn the heat down to medium-low and slowly add the milk mixture to the chowder, stirring constantly.

5 Bring to a simmer and cook until slightly thickened. Taste and adjust the seasonings. Ladle into bowls and sprinkle with the crispy bacon.

RECIPE RIFF

Vegetarian Corn Chowder: Make this recipe vegetarian by omitting the bacon and crab and substituting a few tablespoons of butter for the bacon fat. Serve with cheddar cheese and you've got a delicious corn chowder!

fish cakes with lemon-dill aioli

SERVES 4

PREP: 10 MINUTES, PLUS
10 MINUTES TO COOL AND
5 MINUTES TO MELD

COOK: 25 MINUTES

FOR THE AIOLI

½ cup mayonnaise

Juice and zest of 1 lemon

1 garlic clove, minced

¾ teaspoon dried dill

¼ teaspoon kosher salt

FOR THE FISH CAKES

1½ pounds cod fillets

4 tablespoons olive oil, divided

½ teaspoon paprika

½ teaspoon kosher salt

½ teaspoon Italian seasoning

¼ teaspoon freshly ground black pepper

¼ teaspoon cayenne pepper

½ cup panko bread crumbs

¼ cup mayonnaise

2 tablespoons finely minced onion

Juice of 1 lemon

When I first made this dish, I was surprised by how much my kids loved it! But I shouldn't have been, because these fish cakes are so easy to love. They're crispy on the outside and tender and flaky on the inside. Try serving them alongside baked potatoes and a fresh salad.

1 **To make the aioli:** Combine all the aioli ingredients in a small bowl and mix well. Place the aioli in the refrigerator to chill while you assemble the rest of the meal.

2 **To make the fish cakes:** Preheat the oven to 400°F. Line a baking sheet with foil.

3 Place the cod fillets on the baking sheet and drizzle with 1 tablespoon of oil. In a small bowl, combine the paprika, salt, Italian seasoning, pepper, and cayenne. Sprinkle over the fish.

4 Bake for 10 to 12 minutes, depending on the thickness of the fillets, until the fish is cooked through (it should flake easily when poked with a knife). Allow to cool for 10 minutes.

5 Flake the fish into a large bowl. Add the panko, mayonnaise, onion, and lemon juice. Stir well and set aside for 5 minutes to meld the flavors.

6 In a large nonstick skillet, heat the remaining 3 tablespoons of oil over medium-high heat. Form the fish mixture into patties a bit larger than a golf ball. Place the patties in the skillet and cook until golden brown on each side. Remove them from the pan and serve warm with the aioli.

RECIPE RIFFS

Salmon Cakes: Swap out the cod for skinless salmon fillets and substitute ¼ cup of finely chopped red bell pepper for the onion.

Tuna Cakes: Substitute 3 (5-ounce) cans of drained tuna for the cod and omit the Italian seasoning. Serve with sliced avocado and sriracha mayonnaise.

IN A PINCH: This recipe is very flexible and can be made with almost any type of flaked fish. If the mixture is too sticky, add a bit more panko bread crumbs.

STORAGE TIP: The fish can be cooked ahead of time and stored in the refrigerator for up to 3 days for an even quicker weeknight meal.

crab quiche

SERVES 4 TO 6

PREP: 10 MINUTES, PLUS
10 MINUTES TO STAND

COOK: 40 MINUTES

1 hot, blind-baked Perfect
Piecrust (page 30)

¾ cup shredded cheese,
divided:

- Swiss
- Cheddar
- Mozzarella

1 tablespoon butter

⅓ cup chopped vegetables:

- Bell pepper
- Mushrooms
- Asparagus

3 tablespoons chopped
onion:

- Scallions
- Shallots
- Red onion

1 (6-ounce) can lump
crabmeat, drained

1¼ cups milk

4 large eggs

½ teaspoon kosher salt

½ teaspoon hot sauce

> **STORAGE TIP:** This
> quiche will keep in the
> refrigerator for 3 days.
> Reheat leftovers in the
> microwave, air fryer,
> or a dry skillet over
> medium heat for an
> easy breakfast.

You may think that seafood and eggs is an odd combo, but this quiche will prove you wrong. The contrast between the creamy filling and the crisp crust is fantastic. For brunch, I like to serve this quiche with an easy green salad dressed with Simple Vinaigrette (page 18).

1 Immediately after removing the piecrust from the oven, sprinkle the bottom of the crust with ¼ cup of shredded cheese and set aside.

2 Preheat the oven to 400°F.

3 In a small skillet, melt the butter over medium heat. Add the chopped vegetables and onion and sauté until tender. Arrange the mixture evenly in the crust.

4 Flake the crab and arrange on top of the vegetables.

5 In a bowl, whisk together the milk, eggs, salt, and hot sauce until well combined. Pour evenly into the crust.

6 Bake the quiche for 25 to 30 minutes, until the middle is set. If the edges of the crust are becoming too brown, cover them with strips of aluminum foil. Let stand for 10 minutes before cutting.

RECIPE RIFF

Shrimp Quiche: Substitute canned or cooked small shrimp for the crab. You can also get creative with the vegetables and add whatever you have in your crisper drawer.

spicy shrimp and cheddar grits

SERVES 4

PREP: 15 MINUTES

COOK: 30 MINUTES

FOR THE GRITS

2 cups water

2 cups milk

2 teaspoons kosher salt

¼ teaspoon freshly ground black pepper

1 cup cornmeal

½ cup shredded cheddar cheese

3 tablespoons unsalted butter

FOR THE SHRIMP

8 ounces smoked beef sausage, sliced thinly

½ medium onion, diced

1 tablespoon tomato paste

1 tablespoon all-purpose flour

1 cup vegetable stock

1 (14-ounce) can petite diced tomatoes, undrained

1½ teaspoons kosher salt

½ teaspoon Italian seasoning

¼ teaspoon freshly ground black pepper

¼ teaspoon cayenne pepper

1 pound frozen peeled and deveined shrimp, thawed

Shrimp and grits is one of the greatest Southern comfort foods. The creamy, cheesy grits contrast with the spicy shrimp, and the combination is just perfect. Sliced scallions make a nice garnish, and you can also sprinkle your grits with crispy bacon and hot sauce for even more spice.

1 **To make the grits:** In a saucepan, combine the water, milk, salt, and pepper. Bring to a simmer and slowly whisk in the cornmeal. Cover and continue to cook over low heat for 10 to 15 minutes, whisking frequently, until the mixture is creamy.

2 Remove from the heat, then whisk in the cheddar and butter until combined.

3 **To make the shrimp:** In a large skillet, sauté the sausage and onion over medium heat for 6 to 8 minutes, until lightly browned.

4 Add the tomato paste and flour and cook for 2 to 3 minutes. Whisk in the stock, tomatoes, salt, Italian seasoning, pepper, and cayenne.

5 Bring the mixture to a simmer, then stir in the shrimp. Cover and cook for about 4 minutes, until the shrimp are opaque and cooked through. Season to taste with additional salt and pepper.

6 Place a scoop of grits in a wide, shallow bowl and top with the shrimp mixture.

> **REINVENT IT:** Place leftover grits in a rectangular dish and refrigerate. The next day, cut into squares and crisp in a skillet with some olive oil for a tasty breakfast or side dish.

fish tacos with lime crema

GLUTEN-FREE

SERVES 4

PREP: 10 MINUTES

COOK: 15 MINUTES

FOR THE LIME CREMA

1 cup sour cream

Juice and zest of 1 lime

2 tablespoons water

½ teaspoon kosher salt

FOR THE TACOS

1½ pounds frozen fish, thawed:

- Cod
- Tilapia
- Halibut

1 tablespoon chili powder

2 teaspoons ground cumin

1 teaspoon kosher salt

½ teaspoon freshly ground black pepper

Juice of 1 lime

4 tablespoons unsalted butter

8 (6- to 8-inch) tortillas:

- Corn tortillas
- Flour tortillas

2 cups shredded cheese:

- Cheddar
- Pepper Jack
- Monterey Jack

Lettuce, tomato, onion, cilantro, and salsa, for serving (optional)

Fish tacos are perfect for quick weeknight meals. These ones will be on the table in under 30 minutes! Don't skip the lime crema; it adds a creamy, bright flavor to these tacos.

1 Preheat the oven to 400°F. Line a baking sheet with parchment paper and set aside.

2 **To make the lime crema:** In a bowl, stir together all the crema ingredients and set aside.

3 **To make the tacos:** Place the fish fillets on the prepared baking sheet. Season the fish with the chili powder, cumin, salt, and pepper. Drizzle the lime juice over the fish, then place a pat of butter on top of each fillet. Bake for 10 to 12 minutes, until cooked through. The fish is done when it is firm to the touch and opaque throughout. The timing will depend on the thickness of the fish, so check on the early side if you're using thin fillets.

4 In a dry skillet, warm the tortillas over medium heat until lightly brown.

5 Flake the fish and serve on the tortillas with the cheese, any desired toppings, and the lime crema.

RECIPE RIFF

Shrimp Tacos: Have shrimp on hand instead of fish? Use the same seasoning method, then sauté the shrimp in a skillet with a bit of olive oil or butter.

COOKING TIP: Most store-bought tortillas are meant to be heated. Cooking them in a dry skillet will soften the tortillas while adding a bit of toasty flavor.

shrimp scampi

GLUTEN-FREE

SERVES 4

PREP: 5 MINUTES

COOK: 5 MINUTES

2 tablespoons unsalted butter

2 tablespoons olive oil

1½ pounds raw shrimp

4 garlic cloves, minced

1 cup vegetable stock

1 tablespoon rice wine vinegar

¼ cup grated Parmesan cheese

Kosher salt

Freshly ground black pepper

Shrimp scampi is one of my favorite seafood dishes, and it's surprisingly simple to make. Serve this dish with crusty bread or hot pasta and a side salad for a weeknight meal that's ready in about 10 minutes.

1 In a large skillet, heat the butter and oil over medium-high heat. When the butter is melted, add the shrimp and garlic.

2 Cook the shrimp for 3 to 4 minutes, depending on the size of the shrimp, until just opaque.

3 Add the stock and vinegar, then simmer for about 1 minute. Remove from the heat and sprinkle with the Parmesan. Season to taste with salt and pepper, then serve.

RECIPE RIFF

Sautéed Scallops: Substitute raw scallops for the shrimp, browning on both sides before adding the stock and vinegar.

COOKING TIP: Any size of shrimp can be used for this recipe, but the cook time will vary. Shrimp is done when it is opaque and firm to the touch. Take care not to overcook, or the shrimp will become tough.

cod picatta

DAIRY-FREE

SERVES 4

PREP: 10 MINUTES

COOK: 15 MINUTES

4 tablespoons olive oil, divided

½ cup all-purpose flour

1½ pounds cod fillets

Kosher salt

Freshly ground black pepper

½ teaspoon Italian seasoning

¼ teaspoon cayenne pepper

2 tablespoons capers, drained

2 garlic cloves, minced

Juice of 2 lemons

⅓ cup vegetable stock

You might be more familiar with chicken picatta, which is cooked in a lemony sauce with plenty of capers. However, that sauce is just as delicious with fish! Try serving this dish over hot cooked pasta, rice, or potatoes to absorb even more of the delightful sauce.

1 In a large skillet, heat 2 tablespoons of oil over medium-high heat. Place the flour on a plate.

2 Season both sides of the cod fillets with salt, pepper, Italian seasoning, and cayenne pepper. Dredge the fish in the flour and shake off any excess.

3 Sauté the cod in the skillet for 3 to 4 minutes on each side, until just cooked through. Transfer to a plate and keep warm.

4 Decrease the heat to medium and add the remaining 2 tablespoons of oil to the skillet. When the oil is hot, add the capers and garlic and sauté for 2 to 3 minutes, until fragrant. Pour in the lemon juice and vegetable stock and scrape up any brown bits from the bottom of the pan. Simmer for 2 minutes, then add the cod and any accumulated juices back to the skillet.

5 Heat the fish in the sauce and serve.

IN A PINCH: This recipe is flexible and can be made with many types of seafood, including salmon, tilapia, swordfish, shrimp, or scallops. If you have white wine on hand, substitute that for the vegetable stock.

COOKING TIP: Keep an eye on the cod. If overcooked, it can become tough and rubbery.

tuna pasta with crispy bread crumbs

SERVES 4

PREP: 5 MINUTES

COOK: 25 MINUTES

8 ounces dried spaghetti

2 tablespoons olive oil

2 tablespoons minced onion

4 garlic cloves, minced

2 tablespoons capers, drained

Juice and zest of 2 lemons

1 (14-ounce) can petite diced tomatoes, drained

2 (5-ounce) cans tuna, drained

2 teaspoons Italian seasoning

Kosher salt

Freshly ground black pepper

1 cup shredded mozzarella cheese

2 tablespoons unsalted butter

½ cup panko bread crumbs

Looking for a new way to use canned tuna? This pasta comes together in a flash and is super flavorful. The crispy bread crumb topping brings a nice contrast to the bright flavors of the tender pasta.

1 Bring a large pot of salted water to a boil. Cook the spaghetti for 8 to 10 minutes, until al dente, or per package directions. Drain the spaghetti, reserving 1 cup of the cooking water.

2 In a medium skillet, heat the oil over medium heat. Add the onion, garlic, and capers and sauté for 4 to 6 minutes, until the onions start to soften. Add the lemon juice and zest, tomatoes, tuna, and Italian seasoning. Stir over medium heat until the mixture is heated through. Taste and adjust the seasoning with salt and pepper.

3 Return the spaghetti to the pot and stir in the tuna mixture followed by the mozzarella. Season to taste with salt and pepper, adding some of the reserved cooking water if the pasta is too dry.

4 In a small nonstick skillet, melt the butter over medium heat, then stir in the panko bread crumbs. Sauté for about 5 minutes, until light brown and crispy. Season with salt.

5 Place the pasta on serving dishes and top with the crispy bread crumbs.

COOKING TIP: After adding the tuna mixture to the pasta, you can rinse and wipe the pan out to use for toasting the bread crumbs. It's always better to have fewer dishes to clean!

seafood enchiladas

SERVES 6

PREP: 35 MINUTES

COOK: 40 MINUTES

4 tablespoons unsalted butter, plus more for greasing the casserole dish

¼ cup all-purpose flour

1 cup vegetable stock

1 (10-ounce) can condensed cream of chicken soup

1¾ cups sour cream, divided, plus more for serving

½ cup Speedy Salsa (page 28), plus more for serving

¼ teaspoon kosher salt

1 pound frozen raw shrimp, thawed

1 (8-ounce) can crabmeat, drained

1 teaspoon hot sauce

1½ cups shredded mozzarella cheese, divided

2 tablespoons chopped cilantro, plus more for serving

12 (6-inch) flour tortillas

Shredded lettuce and tomatoes, for serving

I've perfected this recipe over many years from one a coworker passed on to me. This dish takes a bit of time to assemble, but I promise it won't disappoint.

1 Preheat the oven to 350°F. Grease a 9-by-13-inch casserole dish with butter and set aside.

2 In a saucepan, melt 4 tablespoons of butter over medium heat. Whisk in the flour and cook for 2 to 3 minutes. Whisk in the stock and soup, bring to a simmer, and cook for 2 to 3 minutes, until thickened.

3 Remove from the heat, then stir in ¾ cup of sour cream along with the salsa and salt. Set aside.

4 Bring a medium saucepan of water to a boil. Boil the shrimp for 3 to 4 minutes, until pink and opaque. Use a slotted spoon to transfer the shrimp to a plate lined with paper towels.

5 In a large bowl, stir together the remaining 1 cup of sour cream, along with the cooked shrimp, crabmeat, hot sauce, 1 cup of mozzarella cheese, and the cilantro.

6 Spread ¾ cup of the sauce in the prepared casserole dish. Place about ⅓ cup of seafood filling in each tortilla, roll it up, and place it seam-side down in the dish. Top with the remaining sauce and ½ cup of mozzarella cheese.

7 Bake, uncovered, for 30 minutes or until heated through. Serve with sour cream, salsa, lettuce, tomatoes, and additional cilantro.

IN A PINCH: Store-bought salsa or taco sauce can be substituted for the salsa in this recipe. Canned diced green chiles work great as well.

tuna noodle casserole

SERVES 4

PREP: 10 MINUTES

COOK: 35 MINUTES

Butter or oil, for greasing the casserole dish

8 ounces dried spaghetti, broken into thirds

1 (10-ounce) can condensed cream of chicken soup

¾ cup vegetable stock

1½ cups shredded cheddar cheese, divided

½ teaspoon kosher salt

¼ teaspoon freshly ground black pepper

⅛ teaspoon cayenne pepper

½ cup frozen peas, thawed

2 (5-ounce) cans tuna, drained

2 tablespoons unsalted butter, melted

½ cup panko bread crumbs

Tuna casserole is a pantry classic for good reason. In this recipe, I've punched it up with nontraditional spaghetti and a more flavorful sauce. Your family and friends will love it! This recipe also doubles well to feed a crowd.

1 Preheat the oven to 400°F. Grease a 9-by-13-inch casserole dish with butter or oil and set aside.

2 Bring a large pot of salted water to a boil. Cook the spaghetti for 8 to 10 minutes, until al dente, or per the package directions.

3 In a large bowl, whisk together the soup, stock, ¾ cup of the cheddar, salt, pepper, and cayenne. Stir in the cooked spaghetti, peas, and tuna. Place the tuna mixture in the prepared casserole dish, then sprinkle with the remaining cheese.

4 In a small bowl, mix the melted butter and bread crumbs together. Sprinkle over the casserole.

5 Bake for 25 minutes, or until hot and bubbly. Serve.

IN A PINCH: If you're out of bread crumbs, try topping the casserole with crushed potato chips instead.

STORAGE TIP: This casserole can be prepared through step 4 and stored in the refrigerator for 3 to 5 days or frozen for up to 3 months. Let it thaw in the refrigerator before baking.

honey-soy salmon burgers

DAIRY-FREE

SERVES 4

PREP: 15 MINUTES

COOK: 10 MINUTES

1 pound salmon fillets, cut into 1-inch pieces

1 large egg, lightly beaten

⅓ cup panko bread crumbs

3 garlic cloves, minced, divided

4 tablespoons soy sauce, divided

Juice of ½ lime

¼ teaspoon kosher salt

¼ teaspoon freshly ground black pepper

¼ teaspoon cayenne pepper

2 tablespoons honey

½ teaspoon hot sauce

2 tablespoons olive oil

This recipe is a cross between salmon burgers and maple-soy salmon fillets—two of my family's favorite dishes. I typically serve these over Baked Brown Rice (page 32) with a side of broccoli. However, you can also put your burgers on toasted buns or serve them over a bed of greens.

1 In a food processor, pulse the salmon 5 to 7 times, until it is in very fine pieces. Transfer to a large bowl. If you do not have a food processor, dice the salmon into very small pieces. The burgers will not hold together quite as well but will still be delicious.

2 Add the egg, panko, 2 garlic cloves, 2 tablespoons of soy sauce, lime juice, salt, pepper, and cayenne. Stir lightly until the mixture comes together. Form the mixture into 4 patties.

3 Mix the remaining 2 tablespoons of soy sauce, 1 garlic clove, the honey, and hot sauce in a small bowl and set aside.

4 In a large skillet, heat the oil over medium-high heat. Cook the burgers for about 4 minutes on one side. Flip the burgers and brush with the honey-soy mixture. Cook for 4 minutes on the other side, then flip again and brush liberally with the remaining honey-soy mixture. Serve immediately.

COOKING TIP: Arugula dressed with lime juice, olive oil, salt, and pepper makes a great bed for these burgers.

REINVENT IT: Leftover salmon burgers? Break them up the next day over a salad with sesame dressing.

RECIPE RIFF

Honey-Soy Tuna Burgers: Substitute ahi tuna fillets for the salmon. Serve with avocado and sriracha mayonnaise.

Korean-Style Beef Tacos, page 108

cured and frozen meat

This chapter is full of hearty, homestyle meals to please your entire household. I've included a couple filling breakfast recipes along with nontraditional mains, such as Korean-Style Beef Tacos and Ham Croquettes, that will become welcome additions to your dinner rotation! Pantry cooking doesn't have to be boring, and this chapter shows the versatility of a limited list of ingredients.

ham and cheese egg muffins

GLUTEN-FREE

PREP: 10 MINUTES, PLUS 15 MINUTES TO COOL

COOK: 20 MINUTES

Butter or oil, for greasing the muffin tin (optional)

8 ounces cooked ham, diced

8 large eggs

¾ cup sour cream

1¼ cups shredded cheddar cheese, divided

⅓ cup milk

1 teaspoon Dijon mustard

½ teaspoon kosher salt

½ teaspoon hot sauce

¼ teaspoon freshly ground black pepper

A popular café chain sells a version of these egg muffins for almost five dollars a pair! Make a dozen at home for far less and you'll have them on hand all week for breakfast.

1 Preheat the oven to 375°F. Line a 12-cup muffin tin with silicone liners or grease well.

2 Divide the ham evenly among the muffin cups.

3 In a blender, combine the eggs, sour cream, 1 cup of cheddar, milk, mustard, salt, hot sauce, and pepper. Blend on medium-high speed for about 1 minute, until the mixture is smooth and combined.

4 Pour the egg mixture into the muffin cups. Sprinkle with the remaining ¼ cup of cheddar.

5 Bake for 18 to 20 minutes, until the eggs are set and cooked through. Let cool in the pan for 10 to 15 minutes before removing to a cooling rack.

6 Remove the muffin liners and serve immediately, or let cool to room temperature and store in the refrigerator.

Bacon and Gruyère Egg Muffins: Substitute cooked and crumbled bacon for the ham and shredded Gruyère or Swiss cheese for the cheddar.

Sausage and Pepper Egg Muffins: Substitute browned and drained breakfast sausage for the ham. Add ½ cup of finely chopped green bell pepper to the muffin cups in step 2.

Breakfast Sandwiches: These egg muffins are great on a breakfast sandwich! Toast an English muffin and simply place one in between. Add some arugula for a pop of green.

COOKING TIP: Blending the egg mixture gives these muffins a silky-smooth texture, but if you don't have a blender, feel free to whisk the ingredients together until well combined.

ham croquettes

SERVES 4

PREP: 15 MINUTES, PLUS 2
TO 3 HOURS TO CHILL

COOK: 20 MINUTES

FOR THE HAM

1 pound cooked ham, cut
into 1-inch pieces

2 tablespoons unsalted
butter

2 tablespoons all-purpose
flour

¼ teaspoon kosher salt

⅛ teaspoon freshly ground
black pepper

1 cup milk

FOR THE CROQUETTES

1 cup all-purpose flour

1½ cups panko bread
crumbs

2 large eggs

2 tablespoons water

Olive oil, for frying

Kosher salt

*This recipe was passed down to me by my grand-
mother, and I'm excited to share it with you now!
There is a bit of prep work involved, but it's well
worth the effort. I like to serve it with steamed broccoli and mashed potatoes. It makes for a unique
dinner that your family will rave about.*

1   **To make the ham:** In a food processor, pulse the
ham until finely ground. You should have about
2½ cups of ground ham. Remove and place in a
large bowl.

2   In a saucepan, melt the butter over medium heat.
Whisk in the flour, salt, and pepper. Cook for 2 to
3 minutes. Slowly whisk in the milk and bring to a
simmer. Cook over medium heat for 4 to 6 minutes,
until thickened.

3   Pour the sauce over the ham and stir to combine.
Spread the ham mixture onto a plate and cover
with plastic wrap. Refrigerate for 2 to 3 hours until
cold, or for up to 2 days.

4   **To make the croquettes:** When the ham mixture is
completely cold, roll it into small oval-shaped balls
and flatten slightly. Each croquette should be about
the size of a golf ball.

5 Place the flour and panko on separate plates. In a shallow bowl, beat together the eggs and water.

6 In a nonstick skillet, heat ¾ inch of oil over medium-high heat.

7 Roll the croquettes in the flour and shake off the excess. Next, roll in the egg wash, then in the panko. Fry the croquettes in the oil for 2 to 3 minutes on each side, or until golden brown. Drain on a plate lined with paper towels. Sprinkle with salt while hot.

RECIPE RIFF

Ham and Cheese Croquettes: Top the cooked croquettes with Basic Cheese Sauce (page 27).

COOKING TIP: In the spirit of pantry cooking, I've used olive oil in this recipe. However, these croquettes can also be fried in canola or vegetable oil. Either way, be sure that the ham mixture is very cold before forming the croquettes or they will fall apart when frying.

hash brown breakfast bake

GLUTEN-FREE

SERVES 4 TO 6

PREP: 20 MINUTES, PLUS
5 MINUTES TO COOL

COOK: 35 MINUTES

Butter or oil, for greasing
the casserole dish

3 cups frozen shredded
potatoes, thawed

2 tablespoons unsalted
butter, melted

½ teaspoon kosher salt

¼ teaspoon freshly ground
black pepper

3 large eggs

⅔ cup milk

1 cup cooked meat:

- Ham, cooked and diced
- Breakfast sausage,
  browned and crumbled
- Bacon, cooked and
  diced

1 cup shredded cheese:

- Cheddar
- Swiss
- Pepper Jack

¼ cup chopped vegetables:

- Onions
- Bell peppers
- Mushrooms

This recipe is very flexible and combines the best breakfast foods in one dish. If you prefer your vegetables more tender, you can sauté them before mixing them into the egg mixture. Serve this bake with a side of fruit for a meal the whole family will love!

1 Preheat the oven to 425°F. Grease an 8-by-8-inch casserole dish with butter or oil and set aside.

2 In a bowl, toss together the potatoes, butter, salt, and pepper. Press the mixture into the bottom of the dish. Bake for 15 minutes, until lightly browned. Remove from the oven, then reduce the temperature to 350°F.

3 In a medium bowl, whisk together the eggs and milk until well combined. Stir in the cooked meat, cheese, and vegetables. Pour the mixture over the hash brown crust.

4 Bake for 20 minutes, until the eggs are set and the top is golden brown. Allow to cool for 5 minutes before slicing.

REINVENT IT: Leftovers can be warmed and stuffed into a tortilla with salsa for an easy breakfast burrito.

STORAGE TIP: This bake keeps well in the refrigerator for 3 to 5 days. Portion into individual containers for a quick weekday breakfast.

quick and easy stir-fry

DAIRY-FREE

SERVES 4

PREP: 20 MINUTES

COOK: 20 MINUTES

4 tablespoons olive oil, divided

1 pound raw meat or seafood:

- Boneless skinless chicken breast, cut into bite-size pieces
- Frozen shrimp, thawed
- Beef sirloin, sliced into thin strips

Kosher salt

Freshly ground black pepper

3 cups raw vegetables:

- Broccoli florets
- Carrots, peeled and cut into ¼-inch slices
- Bell peppers, cut into strips
- Mushrooms, sliced
- Green cabbage, cut into bite-size pieces

1 small onion, sliced

Stir-Fry Sauce (page 26)

½ cup stir-fry garnish:

- Canned sliced water chestnuts, drained
- Canned bamboo shoots, drained
- Canned baby corn, drained

Baked Brown Rice (page 32), for serving

Stir-fries are crowd-pleasing meals that can be customized to include almost any ingredients you have on hand. For an even quicker weeknight meal, chop all the ingredients ahead of time and store them in the refrigerator until it's time to cook.

1 In a large nonstick skillet, heat 2 tablespoons of oil over medium-high heat. Season the meat or seafood with salt and pepper and sauté for 5 to 7 minutes for chicken or beef, until cooked through, and 3 to 4 minutes for shrimp. Transfer to a plate and wipe out the skillet.

2 Heat the remaining 2 tablespoons of oil over medium heat. Sauté the vegetables and onion until cooked through to your liking. For harder vegetables like broccoli and carrots, add the water to the pan and cover to steam until tender.

3 Return the meat or seafood to the skillet and pour in your desired amount of stir-fry sauce, along with any of the garnishes. Bring to a boil, then reduce the heat and simmer until thickened, 4 to 6 minutes. Taste and adjust the seasoning. Serve hot over the rice.

RECIPE RIFF

Kung Pao Chicken: Make the recipe using chicken, peppers, and water chestnuts. Add 1 heaping tablespoon of chili-garlic paste (such as Huy Fong) to the Stir-Fry Sauce. Stir in ¼ cup of dry roasted peanuts at the end.

COOKING TIP: Proteins and vegetables have different cooking times, so cooking them in separate batches is best. Use as much or as little of the sauce as you like.

chicken salad sandwiches

SERVES 4

PREP: 30 MINUTES

COOK: 15 MINUTES

2 tablespoons olive oil

2 large or 3 small boneless
skinless chicken breasts

Kosher salt

Freshly ground black
pepper

¼ cup water

⅓ cup mayonnaise

¼ cup sour cream

2 tablespoons milk

Juice of 1 lemon

1 tablespoon brown sugar

½ teaspoon dried dill

⅓ cup dried cranberries

⅓ cup chopped walnuts

8 slices hearty white bread,
toasted if desired

Green leaf lettuce, for
serving

I must admit that this classic recipe is one of my favorites in the book! I love a good chicken salad sandwich, and this one is the best. You can also serve the chicken salad on croissants if you're feeling fancy.

1 In a large nonstick skillet, heat the oil over medium-high heat.

2 Season the chicken on both sides with salt and pepper. Sauté the chicken on one side for about 4 minutes, until golden brown. Flip the chicken and sauté for 2 more minutes on the other side, then reduce the heat to medium and add the water. Cover the pan and simmer for 6 to 8 minutes, until the chicken is cooked through. Transfer to a plate and let cool completely.

3 In a bowl, stir together the mayonnaise, sour cream, milk, lemon juice, sugar, and dill.

4 Cut the chicken into bite-size pieces. Stir the chicken, cranberries, and walnuts into the dressing until well combined. Taste and season with salt and pepper.

5 Serve the chicken salad on the bread with lettuce.

STORAGE TIP: The chicken salad keeps well in the refrigerator for up to 3 days. Feel free to make it ahead and simply serve it on bread, crackers, or a lettuce leaf when you're ready to eat.

COOKING TIP: This method of cooking results in tender chicken that isn't dried out. Ensure that the chicken is completely cool before combining it with the dressing. You can even make the chicken ahead of time and store it in the refrigerator until you're ready to use it.

IN A PINCH: If you've already made my Creamy Garlic Dressing (page 20), you can substitute ⅔ cup for the dressing ingredients here.

classic beef chili

DAIRY-FREE · GLUTEN-FREE

SERVES 6 TO 8

PREP: 15 MINUTES

COOK: 40 MINUTES

2 pounds 90-percent lean ground beef

1 small onion, diced

4 cups water

2 (28-ounce) cans crushed tomatoes

1 (14-ounce) can diced tomatoes, undrained

2 (14-ounce) cans pinto beans, drained

5 tablespoons chili powder

2 tablespoons ground cumin

1 tablespoon kosher salt

1 tablespoon granulated sugar

½ teaspoon freshly ground black pepper

½ teaspoon cayenne pepper

Cheese, sour cream, crackers, and chopped onion, for serving (optional)

Chili is a family favorite in my house, and it might just become a beloved dish in yours as well. Make a large pot and keep it warm in the slow cooker to serve a crowd on game day or at a potluck.

1 In a large soup pot, sauté the beef and onion over medium-high heat for 8 to 10 minutes, until the beef is no longer pink. Drain the fat and return to the pot.

2 Stir in the water, crushed tomatoes, diced tomatoes, beans, chili powder, cumin, salt, sugar, pepper, and cayenne. Bring to a boil, then reduce the heat to medium. Simmer for at least 30 minutes.

3 Taste the chili for seasoning and adjust with more salt, pepper, or chili powder. Serve hot with your desired toppings.

RECIPE RIFFS

Chili Mac: Combine 2 cups of the chili with 3 cups of cooked macaroni, then top with shredded cheddar cheese.

Chili Corn Bread Casserole: Place the chili in an oven-safe dish—a cast-iron skillet or deep-dish pie plate works well. Mix 1 package of corn muffin mix according to the package directions and pour on top of the chili. Sprinkle with shredded cheddar cheese and bake as directed on the package, until the corn bread is browned and cooked through.

REINVENT IT: Leftover chili can be used in a variety of ways. Try it on top of a baked potato or hot dog.

chicken potpie

SERVES 4 TO 6

PREP: 25 MINUTES, PLUS
10 MINUTES TO COOL

COOK: 50 MINUTES

4 tablespoons unsalted
butter, plus more for
greasing the pie plate

¼ cup minced onion

2 carrots, diced

¼ cup all-purpose flour

1½ cups vegetable stock

½ cup milk

½ teaspoon Italian
seasoning

½ teaspoon kosher salt

¼ teaspoon freshly ground
black pepper

2 cups cubed, cooked
boneless skinless chicken
breast

1 cup canned corn, drained

1 cup frozen peas

2 batches Perfect Piecrust
(page 30)

This warm, comforting meal can be whipped up with basic ingredients you probably already have in your kitchen. Homemade potpie is easier than you think, and with a creamy filling and flaky crust, this meal is sure to please even the pickiest of eaters.

1 Preheat the oven to 400°F. Grease a 9-inch pie plate with butter and set aside.

2 In a large skillet, melt 4 tablespoons of butter over medium heat. Add the onion and carrots and sauté for 5 minutes, until tender. Stir in the flour, then whisk in the stock, milk, Italian seasoning, salt, and pepper. Simmer for 5 minutes, until thickened. Remove from the heat.

3 Mix the chicken, corn, and peas into the gravy. Set aside to cool slightly.

4 Roll out one batch of the crust and place in the prepared pie plate. Spoon the chicken mixture into the crust and spread evenly. Roll out the second batch of the crust and place it over the filling. Crimp the edges.

5 Cut several slits in the top crust to vent. Place the pie pan on a baking sheet lined with foil to catch any drips. Bake for 35 to 40 minutes, until the pie is golden brown. If the edges get too brown, cover with strips of foil to prevent excessive browning. Let stand for 10 minutes prior to serving.

shepherd's pie

SERVES 6

PREP: 15 MINUTES, PLUS
10 MINUTES TO COOL

COOK: 40 MINUTES

FOR THE POTATOES

Butter or oil, for greasing
the casserole dish

4 medium to large russet
potatoes, peeled and
cubed

½ cup milk

4 tablespoons unsalted
butter

2 teaspoons kosher salt

¼ teaspoon freshly ground
black pepper

FOR THE PIE

1½ pounds 90-percent lean
ground beef

1 small onion, diced

3 carrots, peeled and diced

1 teaspoon kosher salt

½ teaspoon freshly ground
black pepper

½ teaspoon Italian
seasoning

2 tablespoons tomato paste

2 tablespoons all-purpose
flour

1½ cups vegetable stock

1½ cups frozen peas

1 cup shredded cheddar
cheese

*If you're in the mood for some savory comfort food,
this is the meal for you! It combines fluffy, cheesy
potatoes with a rich beef and vegetable filling, perfect
for a cozy weekend dinner.*

1 **To make the potatoes:** Preheat the oven to 400°F.
Grease a 2-quart casserole dish and set aside.

2 Place the potatoes in a large pot of cold water.
Bring to a boil and simmer for 15 minutes, until the
potatoes are very tender. Drain when done, then
return to the pot. Add the milk, butter, salt, and
pepper and mash until creamy. Adjust the seasoning to taste by adding more salt or pepper.

3 **To make the pie:** While the potatoes are boiling, make the beef filling. In a large skillet over
medium-high heat, combine the beef, onion, carrots, salt, pepper, and Italian seasoning and sauté
for 8 to 10 minutes, until the beef is no longer pink.
Stir in the tomato paste and cook for 2 minutes. Stir
in the flour and cook for 2 more minutes.

4 Pour in the stock and bring to a simmer, stirring
frequently. Stir in the peas and allow the mixture
to heat through. Adjust the seasoning to taste by
adding more salt or pepper.

5 Transfer the beef mixture to the prepared casserole dish. Spread the mashed potatoes in an even
layer on top of the beef. Sprinkle the cheddar on
top of the potatoes.

6 Bake for 20 to 25 minutes, until the dish is bubbling and the top is slightly brown. Allow to cool for
10 minutes before serving.

STORAGE TIP: You can make the beef filling ahead of time and store it in the refrigerator for up to 3 days. The entire pie can also be frozen after step 5 and stored in the freezer, tightly wrapped, for up to 3 months. Thaw in the refrigerator before baking.

IN A PINCH: If you're short on time or don't have fresh potatoes on hand, instant mashed potatoes make an easy substitute.

honey-mustard chicken and rice

DAIRY-FREE · GLUTEN-FREE

SERVES 4

PREP: 15 MINUTES

COOK: 25 MINUTES

½ cup mayonnaise

¼ cup Dijon mustard

¼ cup honey

1 tablespoon unseasoned rice vinegar

½ teaspoon kosher salt, plus more for seasoning

⅛ teaspoon freshly ground black pepper, plus more for seasoning

4 boneless skinless chicken breasts

2 tablespoons olive oil

Baked Brown Rice (page 32), for serving

I developed this recipe as a quick way to throw together a flavorful chicken dinner. My kids and husband love this, and it's so easy to make! Try serving it with a salad or steamed vegetables.

1 Preheat the oven to 400°F. In a small casserole dish, whisk together the mayonnaise, mustard, honey, vinegar, salt, and pepper until combined. Cover with foil and place in the oven while it preheats.

2 Season the chicken on both sides with salt and pepper. In a nonstick skillet, heat the oil over medium-high heat. Sauté the chicken for 3 to 4 minutes on each side, until golden brown.

3 Remove the chicken from the skillet and place it directly into the casserole dish with the honey-mustard sauce, turning to coat. Cover again with the foil and place it back in the oven.

4 Bake for 10 to 15 minutes longer, until the chicken is cooked through. Serve chicken and sauce on top of the rice.

RECIPE RIFF

Honey-Mustard Pork Chops: Follow the recipe as directed, substituting boneless pork loin chops for the chicken breast.

IN A PINCH: Any type of mustard can be used in place of the Dijon, including yellow mustard.

slow-cooker creamy chicken chili

GLUTEN-FREE

SERVES 6 TO 8

PREP: 10 MINUTES

COOK: 4 TO 8 HOURS

3 medium to large boneless skinless chicken breasts

3 cups vegetable stock

1 (15-ounce) can corn, undrained

1 (15-ounce) can pinto beans, rinsed and drained

1 (15-ounce) can diced tomatoes, undrained

2 garlic cloves, minced

1 tablespoon chili powder

2 teaspoons ground cumin

1 teaspoon hot sauce

¾ teaspoon dried dill

1 teaspoon kosher salt

½ teaspoon freshly ground black pepper

1 (8-ounce) package cream cheese

1 cup shredded cheddar cheese

STORAGE TIP: If you're looking to prep a quick freezer meal, combine all the ingredients except the cheddar in a gallon-size freezer bag and freeze for up to 3 months. Partially thaw before cooking as directed.

This chili cooks for several hours in a slow cooker, but it only takes a few minutes to put together with ingredients you probably already have on hand. My whole family loves it topped with additional cheese, cilantro, and sour cream with a side of tortilla chips for dipping.

1 Place the chicken breasts in a slow cooker. Pour in the stock, corn, beans, tomatoes, garlic, chili powder, cumin, hot sauce, dill, salt, and pepper. Stir to combine.

2 Place the cream cheese on top of the mixture. Cover and cook on high for 4 hours or low for 8 hours.

3 Transfer the chicken to a plate and allow to cool slightly. Using a whisk, stir the remaining mixture in the slow cooker to ensure the cream cheese is incorporated and no lumps remain. Stir in the cheddar.

4 Using 2 forks, shred the chicken into bite-size pieces and return to the slow cooker. Stir to combine.

5 Serve the chili in bowls with your preferred toppings.

RECIPE RIFFS

Creamy Chicken Nachos: This chili is extra special served alongside or on top of nachos! Simply drain off some of the broth before topping the chips.

Creamy Beef Chili: Substitute 1 pound of ground beef, cooked and drained, for the chicken breast.

butter chicken

GLUTEN-FREE

SERVES 4

PREP: 10 MINUTES, PLUS
AT LEAST 30 MINUTES TO
MARINATE

COOK: 35 MINUTES

FOR THE MARINADE

1 cup sour cream

Juice of 1 lemon

2 teaspoons turmeric

2 teaspoons ground cumin

1½ teaspoons garam masala

1 teaspoon kosher salt

1½ pounds boneless
skinless chicken breasts,
cut into bite-size pieces

FOR THE CHICKEN

2 tablespoons olive oil

4 garlic cloves, minced

1 cup vegetable stock

1 (14-ounce) can diced
tomatoes, undrained

1 teaspoon paprika

1 teaspoon kosher salt

½ teaspoon turmeric

½ teaspoon garam masala

½ teaspoon ground cumin

½ teaspoon hot sauce

3 tablespoons unsalted
butter, cut into cubes

½ cup full-fat coconut milk

Traditional butter chicken originated in India and is smothered in a spiced tomato, butter, and cream sauce. You can make my spin on this tasty dish with just pantry staples. My recipe calls for a long list of ingredients, but half of them are spices, and the flavor of the end dish is well worth it. It's perfect topped with chopped cilantro over Baked Brown Rice (page 32), or with a side of naan to soak up the sauce.

1 **To make the marinade:** In a bowl, combine the sour cream, lemon juice, turmeric, cumin, garam masala, and salt. Whisk to combine, then stir in the chicken. Refrigerate for at least 30 minutes, or up to 24 hours.

2 **To make the chicken:** In a large skillet, heat the oil over medium-high heat. Add the garlic and sauté for 2 minutes, until fragrant. Add the chicken and marinade to the pan and cook for about 4 minutes.

3 Stir in the stock, tomatoes, paprika, salt, turmeric, garam masala, cumin, and hot sauce. Bring to a simmer, then reduce the heat to medium. Cover and cook for 20 to 25 minutes, stirring frequently to avoid sticking.

4 Remove the lid and stir the butter into the sauce until melted. Stir in the coconut milk. Adjust the seasoning to taste by adding more salt.

COOKING TIP: Marinating the chicken in sour cream and lemon juice helps to tenderize it. The longer you can let it marinate, the more tender it will be.

thai-inspired shredded pork

DAIRY-FREE

SERVES 6

PREP: 10 MINUTES

COOK: 4 TO 8 HOURS

1 (2-pound) pork loin roast, trimmed of excess fat

Kosher salt

Freshly ground black pepper

1 onion, sliced

4 garlic cloves, minced

2 teaspoons hot sauce

½ cup vegetable stock

¼ cup soy sauce

2 tablespoons brown sugar

2 tablespoons unseasoned rice vinegar

½ cup creamy peanut butter

Baked Brown Rice (page 32), for serving

2 limes, cut into wedges

½ cup chopped cilantro

This pork is extremely tender and moist after cooking in the slow cooker all day. The combination of salty soy sauce, sweet peanut butter, and tangy vinegar brings traditional Thai flavors to this recipe. Try serving it with rice noodles or on top of Baked Brown Rice (page 32).

1 Place the pork roast in a slow cooker. Season with salt and pepper, then top with the onion, garlic, and hot sauce. In a small bowl, whisk together the stock, soy sauce, sugar, and vinegar. Pour over the pork.

2 Cover and cook on high for 4 hours or low for 8 hours. Remove the pork from the slow cooker and place it on a cutting board. Whisk the peanut butter into the sauce in the slow cooker.

3 Cut the pork into thick slices or shred it into large pieces. Return the pork to the sauce.

4 Serve the pork over the rice and top with the lime wedges and cilantro.

RECIPE RIFF

Slow Cooker Thai-Style Chicken: Substitute 3 or 4 large boneless skinless chicken breasts for the pork roast and follow the recipe as directed.

COOKING TIP: If you're cooking for someone with a gluten sensitivity, make this recipe gluten-free by swapping the soy sauce for tamari.

korean-style beef tacos

SERVES 4

PREP: 10 MINUTES

COOK: 15 MINUTES

FOR THE BEEF

1 pound 90-percent lean ground beef

½ small yellow onion, finely minced

2 garlic cloves, minced

3 tablespoons soy sauce

3 tablespoons brown sugar

Juice of 1 lime

2 teaspoons sesame oil

½ teaspoon hot sauce

FOR THE TACOS

½ cup sour cream

Juice of 1 lime

1 teaspoon hot sauce

¼ teaspoon kosher salt

8 to 10 (6-inch) flour tortillas

Fresh chopped cilantro, for serving

For this nontraditional take on tacos, I was inspired by Korean recipes for beef. In my creation, a salty beef filling contrasts with a cool sour cream sauce for a fantastic combination of flavors. When you're tired of the same old taco night, try these instead!

1 **To make the beef:** In a large skillet, sauté the beef, onion, and garlic over medium-high heat for 6 to 8 minutes, until the beef is cooked through. Drain the fat.

2 In a small bowl, whisk together the soy sauce, sugar, lime juice, oil, and hot sauce. Stir into the beef and cook over medium heat for about 4 minutes, until heated through. Remove from the heat and set aside.

3 **To make the tacos:** In a small bowl, whisk together the sour cream, lime juice, hot sauce, and salt.

4 In a dry skillet, toast the tortillas over medium heat until just starting to brown on both sides. Serve the beef filling in the tortillas topped with the sour cream sauce and cilantro.

> **RECIPE RIFF**
>
> **Korean-Style Beef and Rice:** If you're not in the mood for tacos or don't have tortillas on hand, make a batch of Baked Brown Rice (page 32) and serve topped with the beef, sour cream sauce, and cilantro.

> **COOKING TIP:** If you have some on hand, kimchi is also a great topping for these tacos.

Lemon Squares, page 128

baking staples

In this chapter, you'll find all types of baking recipes, including both sweet and savory. Breakfast recipes like Classic Crepes and Sour Cream Coffee Cake will get your day started out right, while versatile snacks and sides such as Focaccia and Pepperoni Rolls will round out your meals. Recipes like Chocolate Chip Blondies and Lemon Squares will also satisfy your sweet tooth.

cream cheese danishes

YIELD: 16 SMALL DANISHES
PREP: 20 MINUTES
COOK: 15 MINUTES

1 (8-ounce) package cream cheese, softened

¼ cup plus 2 tablespoons granulated sugar

1 egg yolk

2 tablespoons lemon juice

1 teaspoon vanilla extract

1 (8-ounce) tube crescent rolls

2 tablespoons unsalted butter, melted

2 tablespoons brown sugar

You'll be amazed by how easy these danishes are to make at home! Using premade crescent rolls is a handy shortcut that saves time and effort but doesn't compromise on flavor. Enjoy these danishes for dessert, brunch, or breakfast.

1 Preheat the oven to 350°F. Line a baking sheet with parchment paper and set aside.

2 In a large bowl, combine the cream cheese and sugar and use an electric mixer to beat until smooth. Add the egg yolk, mixing well. Mix in the lemon juice and vanilla and beat until smooth.

3 Remove the crescent rolls from the tube but do not unroll them. Using a sharp knife, slice the rolls into 16 equal rounds. Place the rounds on the baking sheet and use your fingers to flatten the center, creating a well in the center of each roll.

4 Brush the rolls with the butter and sprinkle with the brown sugar. Place about 2 tablespoons of filling into the well in each roll. Bake for 15 to 16 minutes, until the rolls are light golden brown.

5 Let cool to room temperature before serving.

RECIPE RIFFS

Cherry and Cheese Danishes: Top the cream cheese mixture with 1 tablespoon of cherry pie filling before baking.

Almond Danishes: Replace the vanilla with almond extract. Before baking, sprinkle slivered almonds over the filling.

mix and match muffins

VEGETARIAN

SERVES 12

PREP: 15 MINUTES, PLUS
10 MINUTES TO COOL

COOK: 25 MINUTES

2 cups all-purpose flour

⅔ cup granulated sugar

2 teaspoons baking powder

½ teaspoon kosher salt

2 large eggs

¾ cup milk

4 tablespoons unsalted butter, melted and cooled slightly

Muffin mix-ins:

- 1 cup fresh blueberries
- 1 apple, peeled and finely diced, tossed with 1 tablespoon sugar and ½ teaspoon ground cinnamon
- 1 cup semi sweet chocolate chips
- 2 mashed bananas, ¼ cup peanut butter, and ⅓ cup chocolate chips

Once you master the basic muffin formula, the possibilities are endless. Stir in whatever you have on hand for a quick snack or breakfast throughout the week. Feel free to try one of my recommended mix-ins, or dream up your own flavor combinations.

1 Preheat the oven to 400°F. Place paper liners in a 12-cup muffin tin.

2 In a large bowl, whisk together the flour, sugar, baking powder, and salt. In a separate bowl, whisk together the eggs, milk, and butter. Pour the wet ingredients into the dry and stir until just combined.

3 Stir in your choice of muffin mix-ins. Scoop the batter into the muffin liners.

4 Bake for 18 to 22 minutes, until golden brown and a toothpick inserted into a muffin comes out mostly clean. Take care not to overbake or the muffins will be tough.

5 Allow to cool in the pan for 5 to 10 minutes. Remove to a wire rack and let cool completely.

COOKING TIP: I keep coarse turbinado sugar on hand specifically for baking. Sprinkle a bit on top of each muffin before they go in the oven for a sweet crunch that mimics bakery muffins.

STORAGE TIP: These muffins will keep in an airtight container for up to 3 days. They can also be frozen for up to 6 weeks.

sour cream coffee cake

VEGETARIAN

SERVES 8

PREP: 20 MINUTES

COOK: 45 MINUTES

FOR THE CAKE

8 tablespoons unsalted butter, at room temperature, plus more for greasing the pan

¾ cup granulated sugar

1 large egg

¾ cup sour cream

1 teaspoon vanilla extract

1 cup all-purpose flour

1 teaspoon baking powder

½ teaspoon kosher salt

FOR THE CRUMB TOPPING

4 tablespoons cold unsalted butter, diced

¼ cup brown sugar

1 teaspoon ground cinnamon

2 tablespoons all-purpose flour

This coffee cake has a tender and moist crumb, thanks to the addition of sour cream in the batter. A slice pairs perfectly with a hot cup of coffee or tea. Try serving it in a brunch spread, as a quick snack, or for an indulgent breakfast.

1 **To make the cake:** Preheat the oven to 350°F. Grease an 8-by-8-inch pan and set aside.

2 In a bowl, cream the butter and sugar with an electric mixture for about 2 minutes, until light and fluffy. Add the egg and stir until combined. Stir in the sour cream and vanilla until combined, scraping down the sides as needed.

3 In a medium bowl, whisk together the flour, baking powder, and salt. Add slowly to the wet ingredients and mix until combined. Spread half of the batter in the prepared pan.

4 **To make the crumb topping:** Combine all the crumb topping ingredients together in a bowl and mix with a fork or pastry cutter until the mixture is crumbly and the pieces of butter are the size of peas. Sprinkle half of the topping over the batter in the pan, then top with the remaining batter.

5 Sprinkle the remaining crumb topping on the cake. Bake for 40 to 45 minutes, until a toothpick inserted in the center comes out mostly clean.

6 Let cool to room temperature, cut into squares, and serve.

RECIPE RIFF

Almond Coffee Cake: Add 1 teaspoon of almond extract to the batter along with the vanilla. Add ½ cup of slivered almonds to the topping.

COOKING TIP: Layering the batter with the crumb topping gives this coffee cake a sweet ribbon of cinnamon flavor throughout.

foolproof pizza crust

DAIRY-FREE · VEGAN

SERVES 4

PREP: 1 HOUR 20 MINUTES

COOK: 15 MINUTES

½ teaspoon active dry yeast

¾ cup warm water (110°F)

5 tablespoons olive oil, plus more for greasing the bowl

2 cups all-purpose flour, plus more for dusting

¾ teaspoon kosher salt

Cornmeal, for dusting the pan

Pizza crust is surprisingly easy to make at home and tastes so much better than store-bought! This dough comes together quickly and can be stored in the refrigerator for a spontaneous pizza night that's faster than delivery.

1 In a small bowl, stir the yeast into the water until it dissolves. Let stand for 5 minutes. Meanwhile, grease a large bowl with oil and set aside.

2 In a food processor, combine the flour and salt. Add the oil and pulse to combine. Add the yeast mixture and process until the dough forms a ball, then blend 1 minute more.

3 Turn the dough out onto a lightly floured surface and knead until smooth. Place the dough in the oiled bowl, turning to lightly grease the top of the dough. Cover with a kitchen towel or plastic wrap and let rise in a warm, draft-free spot for 1 hour, until doubled.

4 To bake, preheat the oven to 475°F. Roll out the dough and place it on a baking sheet sprinkled with cornmeal. Top as desired and bake for 12 to 15 minutes.

Stromboli: Instead of topping the pizza with sauce, sprinkle the dough with cheese and toppings and roll it up into a log. Place it on a baking sheet, brush with beaten egg, and sprinkle with salt. Bake until golden brown. Slice and serve with Marinara Sauce (page 24).

Calzones: Divide the dough into fourths. Roll each portion into a 6- to 8-inch circle. Fill each circle with 2 tablespoons of Marinara Sauce (page 24) and your choice of meat, cheese, and vegetables. Fold into a half circle and crimp the edges. With a sharp knife, make a slash in each calzone to allow steam to vent. Brush with beaten egg and bake until golden brown. Serve with more Marinara Sauce.

STORAGE TIP: The dough can be prepared in advance and stored in the refrigerator, tightly wrapped, for up to 3 days.

focaccia

DAIRY-FREE · VEGAN

SERVES 6

PREP: 1 HOUR 20 MINUTES

COOK: 20 MINUTES

2¼ teaspoons active dry yeast

¾ cup warm water (110°F)

3 tablespoons olive oil, plus more for greasing the bowl and pan and brushing

2 cups all-purpose flour, plus more for dusting

1½ teaspoons kosher salt, divided

¼ teaspoon Italian seasoning

If you're new to baking with yeast, focaccia is a great bread to start with. You can mix it up in a food processor, and it only requires one rise. In just a couple hours, you'll have soft, delicious bread that goes well with soup or stew.

1 In a small bowl, stir the yeast into the water until it dissolves. Let stand for 5 minutes. Meanwhile, grease a large bowl with oil and set aside.

2 In a food processor, combine the flour and 1 teaspoon of salt. Add the oil and pulse to combine. Add the yeast mixture and process until the dough forms a ball, then blend 1 minute more.

3 Turn the dough out onto a lightly floured surface and knead until smooth. Place the dough in the oiled bowl, turning to lightly grease the top of the dough. Cover with a kitchen towel or plastic wrap and let rise in a warm, draft-free spot for 1 hour, until doubled.

4 Preheat the oven to 425°F. Punch the dough down, then let it rest for 5 minutes. Meanwhile, grease an 8-by-8-inch pan.

5 Fit the dough into the pan and use your fingertips to create dimples in about 12 places. Brush with oil and sprinkle with the remaining ½ teaspoon of salt and the Italian seasoning. Bake for 18 to 20 minutes, until golden brown.

6 Remove the bread from the pan and let cool for several minutes on a wire rack. Cut into rectangles and serve.

RECIPE RIFFS

Parmesan Focaccia: Omit the Italian seasoning. After brushing the dough with oil, top the unbaked focaccia with ⅓ cup of grated Parmesan and sprinkle with black pepper. Bake as directed.

Olive and Sun-Dried Tomato Focaccia: After seasoning the top of the focaccia, arrange drained sun-dried tomatoes and sliced Kalamata olives on top of the dough. Bake as directed.

Cheddar Everything Focaccia: Omit the Italian seasoning. After brushing the dough with oil, top the unbaked focaccia with ⅓ cup of shredded sharp cheddar cheese and sprinkle with everything bagel seasoning.

COOKING TIP: A stand mixer with a paddle attachment can also be used for this recipe.

essential pancakes

VEGETARIAN

SERVES 4

PREP: 15 MINUTES

COOK: 15 MINUTES

2 cups milk

1 tablespoon lemon juice

2 cups all-purpose flour

3 tablespoons granulated sugar

1½ teaspoons baking powder

½ teaspoon kosher salt

2 large eggs

4 tablespoons unsalted butter, melted and cooled slightly

1 teaspoon vanilla extract

Butter or oil, for greasing the griddle

I've been making this pancake recipe for years, and it's a family favorite! I hope your family loves it as well. Pancakes make a great breakfast when you're running low on groceries; you likely have all the ingredients on hand, and you can mix in any leftover fruit that needs to be used up.

1 Combine the milk and lemon juice and set aside for 10 minutes.

2 In a large bowl, whisk together the flour, sugar, baking powder, and salt. In a separate bowl, whisk together the milk mixture with the eggs, butter, and vanilla. Combine the wet and dry ingredients and stir until combined.

3 Preheat a greased griddle or large nonstick skillet over medium heat. Pour the batter onto the griddle in ¼-cup portions. Cook the pancakes until the edges are bubbling and the bottoms are golden brown. Flip and cook on the other side until golden brown.

COOKING TIP: Keep the cooked pancakes warm in a 250°F oven until ready to serve.

SUBSTITUTION TIP: If you don't have a lemon on hand, you can substitute white vinegar for the lemon juice.

RECIPE RIFFS

Blueberry Pancakes: Add ½ teaspoon of ground cinnamon to the batter. After pouring the batter on the griddle, place 4 or 5 blueberries on each pancake before flipping.

Banana-Walnut Pancakes: Mash 2 small, very ripe bananas with a fork and stir them into the batter. After pouring the batter on the griddle, sprinkle each pancake with a few chopped walnuts before flipping.

Pumpkin Pancakes: Add ¾ cup of pumpkin puree and ¼ teaspoon each of ground nutmeg and ground cinnamon to the batter. Serve with maple syrup.

garlic cheese sticks

VEGETARIAN

SERVES 4 TO 6

PREP: 50 MINUTES

COOK: 15 MINUTES

FOR THE DOUGH

2½ cups all-purpose flour, plus more for dusting

1 tablespoon active dry yeast

1 teaspoon kosher salt

1 teaspoon granulated sugar

1 cup very warm water (115°F)

1 tablespoon olive oil, plus more for greasing the bowl

FOR THE CHEESE STICKS

2 tablespoons cornmeal

4 tablespoons unsalted butter, melted

3 tablespoons grated Parmesan cheese

3 garlic cloves, minced

¾ teaspoon Italian seasoning

¼ teaspoon kosher salt

2 cups shredded mozzarella cheese

Marinara Sauce (page 24), for serving (optional)

When we order pizza, one of my favorite things to get is cheese sticks. With this easy recipe, you can make them at home! Serve them alongside a homemade pizza made with my Foolproof Pizza Crust (page 116), or as a side to any pasta dish.

1 **To make the dough:** In a large bowl, whisk together the flour, yeast, salt, and sugar. In a separate bowl, whisk together the water and oil. Pour into the dry ingredients and stir until the mixture forms a ball.

2 Turn the dough out onto a lightly floured surface and knead until smooth, about 3 minutes. Grease a bowl with oil. Place the dough in the oiled bowl, turning to coat the top. Let rise in a warm place for 30 minutes, or until doubled in size.

3 **To make the cheese sticks:** Preheat the oven to 450°F. Sprinkle the cornmeal on a pizza pan or baking sheet.

4 In a small bowl, whisk together the butter, Parmesan, garlic, Italian seasoning, and salt.

5 Spread the dough out on the pan, in a 12-inch circle or oval. Brush the garlic-butter topping evenly over the dough. Sprinkle with the mozzarella.

6 Bake for 13 to 15 minutes, until golden brown and cheese is melted. Cut into strips and serve.

COOKING TIP: A stand mixer with a dough hook can also be used for this recipe.

pepperoni rolls

YIELD: 12 ROLLS

PREP: 20 MINUTES, PLUS
10 MINUTES TO COOL

COOK: 15 MINUTES

1 (8-ounce) can crescent roll dough

All-purpose flour, for dusting

½ cup Marinara Sauce (page 24)

1 cup shredded mozzarella cheese

2 ounces pepperoni, diced

2 tablespoons unsalted butter, melted

2 tablespoons grated Parmesan cheese

These quick rolls satisfy that pizza craving without all the effort. My kids love these for a quick lunch or after-school snack. Try serving them with Ranch Dressing (page 20) or extra Marinara Sauce (page 24) for dipping.

1 Preheat the oven to 350°F. Line a large baking sheet with parchment paper and set aside.

2 Turn the crescent roll dough out onto a lightly floured surface. Using a floured rolling pin, lightly flatten the dough, pressing the seams together.

3 Spread the marinara sauce over the dough, then top with the mozzarella and pepperoni. Starting on the longest side, roll the dough tightly into a log and cut into 12 rolls.

4 Place the rolls on the pan about 2 inches apart. Brush with the butter and sprinkle with the Parmesan. Bake for 14 to 16 minutes, until golden brown.

5 Allow to cool for 10 minutes before serving.

RECIPE RIFFS

Supreme Pizza Rolls: After placing the pepperoni on the dough, top with chopped onion, bell pepper, and sliced black olives. Roll and bake as directed.

Spinach and Artichoke Rolls: Omit the Marinara Sauce and replace with Alfredo Sauce (page 23). Omit the pepperoni and instead sprinkle the dough with ½ cup of finely chopped artichoke hearts and 1 cup of chopped raw spinach. Continue with the recipe as directed. Serve with extra Alfredo Sauce, if desired.

classic crepes

VEGETARIAN

SERVES 6

PREP: 10 MINUTES

COOK: 10 MINUTES

1½ cups milk

2 tablespoons granulated sugar

2 large eggs

1 tablespoon butter, melted and slightly cooled

1 teaspoon vanilla extract

1 cup all-purpose flour

Butter or oil, for greasing the skillet

Many people fear that crepes are fussy and hard to make, but the opposite is true! I like to serve these for breakfast, either spread with Nutella or filled with strawberries and topped with whipped cream.

1 In a large bowl, whisk together the milk, sugar, eggs, butter, and vanilla until well combined. Gradually whisk in the flour until the mixture is smooth.

2 Grease a small nonstick skillet and preheat it over medium heat. Pour 3 tablespoons of crepe batter into the skillet, then quickly lift and tilt the skillet to spread the batter evenly into a circle.

3 Cook until light golden brown, then carefully flip and cook the other side until golden. Remove to a plate and keep warm while preparing the remaining crepes.

RECIPE RIFFS

Savory Crepes: Omit the sugar and vanilla, and add ¼ teaspoon of salt. Cook as directed and fill with meats, eggs, vegetables, or cheese. Almost any combination is delicious topped with hollandaise sauce!

Strawberry Cheesecake Crepes: Beat together 8 ounces of room-temperature cream cheese, ½ cup of powdered sugar, ¼ cup of milk, and 1 teaspoon of vanilla extract until smooth. Fill the crepes with the cheesecake mixture and top with sliced strawberries.

STORAGE TIP: Leftover crepes reheat beautifully. Store in the refrigerator with squares of wax paper layered between the crepes. Reheat in the microwave for 30 seconds.

apple crisp

VEGETARIAN

SERVES 6

PREP: 15 MINUTES, PLUS
20 MINUTES TO COOL

COOK: 40 MINUTES

FOR THE APPLE FILLING

Butter or oil, for greasing
the baking dish

5 apples, peeled and
chopped into ½-inch
pieces

⅓ cup walnuts (optional)

⅓ cup all-purpose flour

½ cup brown sugar

2 tablespoons honey

Juice of 1 lemon

FOR THE CRISP

⅓ cup rolled oats

⅓ cup all-purpose flour

⅓ cup brown sugar

5 tablespoons unsalted
butter, softened

¼ teaspoon ground
cinnamon

¼ teaspoon kosher salt

¼ cup walnuts (optional)

> **STORAGE TIP:** You can
> store any leftovers in
> the refrigerator for 2 to
> 3 days. They reheat well
> in the oven.

Apple Crisp is the ideal pantry-based dessert: It uses basic ingredients I always seem to have hand, and other fruits can be substituted for the apples, depending on what you need to use up. Serve it warm with a scoop of vanilla ice cream for extra indulgence.

1 **To make the apple filling:** Preheat the oven to 375°F. Grease an 8-by-8-inch baking dish or deep-dish pie plate and set aside.

2 In a large bowl, combine the apples, walnuts (if using), flour, sugar, honey, and lemon juice. Stir well, then pour into the prepared baking dish.

3 **To make the crisp:** In a medium bowl, combine the oats, flour, sugar, butter, cinnamon, and salt. Using a pastry cutter or a fork, mix until crumbly. Stir in the walnuts (if using).

4 Sprinkle the topping over the apples and bake for 35 to 40 minutes, until the apples are tender and the top is brown and crisp. Allow to cool for 15 to 20 minutes before serving.

RECIPE RIFFS

Peach Crisp: Substitute peaches for the apples. To peel peaches, cut an x in the bottom of each peach. Place them in boiling water for 1 minute, then transfer to an ice bath to cool. The skins will easily peel off.

Pear Crisp: Substitute peeled and chopped pears for the apples. Add ¼ teaspoon of ground cinnamon to the filling mixture.

chewy oatmeal cookies

VEGETARIAN

YIELD: 24 COOKIES

PREP: 10 MINUTES,

PLUS 5 MINUTES TO COOL

COOK: 15 MINUTES

12 tablespoons unsalted butter, at room temperature

1 cup packed brown sugar

½ cup granulated sugar

1 large egg

1 teaspoon vanilla extract

1¾ cups all-purpose flour

1¼ teaspoons baking powder

2 cups rolled oats

These chewy cookies are irresistible—you won't be able to stop at just one! This recipe is tasty as-is, but you can also customize it by adding raisins or chocolate chips.

1 Preheat the oven to 375°F. Line 2 baking sheets with parchment paper and set aside.

2 In a mixing bowl, combine the butter, brown sugar, and granulated sugar and beat with an electric mixer for 2 to 3 minutes, until light and fluffy. Add the egg and vanilla and mix until just combined.

3 In a separate bowl, whisk together the flour and baking powder, then add to the butter mixture slowly while the mixer is running. Add the oats and mix until just combined.

4 Drop rounded tablespoons of the batter onto the prepared baking sheets about 2 inches apart. Bake for 11 to 13 minutes, or until the edges are lightly browned. Allow to cool on the baking sheets for 5 minutes, then remove to cooling racks.

RECIPE RIFFS

Oatmeal-Raisin Cookies: Add ½ teaspoon of ground cinnamon to the flour mixture. Fold in 1 cup of raisins with the oatmeal. Bake as directed.

Chocolate Chip–Oatmeal Cookies: Add 1½ cups of chocolate chips to the batter along with the oatmeal. Bake as directed.

sour cream sugar cookies

VEGETARIAN

YIELD: 24 COOKIES

PREP: 10 MINUTES, PLUS
1 TO 2 HOURS TO CHILL
AND 5 MINUTES TO COOL

COOK: 15 MINUTES

1½ cups granulated sugar, divided

8 tablespoons unsalted butter, at room temperature

½ cup sour cream

1 large egg

1¾ cups all-purpose flour

2 teaspoons baking powder

¼ teaspoon kosher salt

These soft and scrumptious sugar cookies are less fussy than cut-out cookies but don't sacrifice the flavor. Though you'll need to chill the cookies for an hour or two before baking, the dough only takes a few minutes to mix up.

1 In a large bowl, combine 1 cup of sugar and the butter. Cream with an electric mixer for 2 to 3 minutes, until light and fluffy. Mix in the sour cream and egg until well combined.

2 In a separate bowl, whisk together the flour, baking powder, and salt. Gradually add the dry ingredients to the wet until the dough is well combined, scraping down the sides as needed. Refrigerate until firm, 1 to 2 hours.

3 Preheat the oven to 375°F. Line 2 baking sheets with parchment paper.

4 Roll the dough into balls, about 2 tablespoons of dough for each cookie. Place the remaining ½ cup of sugar in a bowl and roll the cookies in the sugar. Place on the baking sheets 2 inches apart, then flatten slightly.

5 Bake for 9 to 12 minutes, until the bottoms are lightly browned.

6 Let cool on the pans for 5 minutes, then move the cookies to cooling racks.

RECIPE RIFFS

Almond Sugar Cookies: Add ½ teaspoon of almond extract to the dough and sprinkle slivered almonds on top of the cookies before baking.

Festive Holiday Sugar Cookies: Roll the cookies in colored sugar sprinkles before baking. Try using red and green for Christmas or pink and yellow for Easter!

STORAGE TIP: These cookies can be assembled through step 4 and flash-frozen on trays. Store in a zip-top freezer bag and bake from frozen whenever a cookie craving strikes!

lemon squares

VEGETARIAN

Butter or oil, for greasing the pan

1 cup all-purpose flour

8 tablespoons unsalted butter, at room temperature

1¼ cups granulated sugar, divided

Zest of 1 lemon

3 tablespoons lemon juice

2 large eggs

½ teaspoon baking powder

¼ teaspoon kosher salt

These treats are a cinch to make and have such a bright, fresh flavor. If you have powdered sugar on hand, you can dust a little over the top before serving to dress them up.

1 Preheat the oven to 350°F. Grease an 8-by-8-inch pan with butter or oil and set aside.

2 In a small bowl, mix together the flour, butter, and ¼ cup of sugar until well combined. Press the dough into the prepared pan in an even layer. Bake for 20 minutes.

3 Whisk the remaining 1 cup of sugar, lemon zest, lemon juice, eggs, baking powder, and salt in a bowl until light and fluffy. Pour over the hot crust.

4 Bake for 20 minutes, until the top is lightly browned. Let cool completely, then cut into squares.

RECIPE RIFFS

Lemon-Coconut Squares: Add ½ cup of flaked coconut to the filling before baking.

Lemon-Blueberry Squares: Sprinkle ½ cup of fresh blueberries over the lemon filling before baking. Dust with powdered sugar before serving.

STORAGE TIP: Store any leftovers in the refrigerator for 2 to 3 days.

chocolate chip blondies

VEGETARIAN

SERVES 9

PREP: 15 MINUTES

COOK: 35 MINUTES

Butter or oil, for greasing the pan

1 cup all-purpose flour

½ teaspoon kosher salt

¼ teaspoon baking powder

1 cup packed brown sugar

8 tablespoons unsalted butter, melted and cooled slightly

1 large egg

1 teaspoon vanilla extract

½ cup semisweet chocolate chips

This recipe couldn't be simpler to put together and is a nice change from brownies. It makes an even more decadent dessert when served warm with a scoop of vanilla ice cream.

1 Preheat the oven to 350°F. Grease an 8-by-8-inch pan with butter or oil and line it with parchment paper. Set aside.

2 In a small bowl, whisk together the flour, salt, and baking powder.

3 In a separate bowl, stir together the brown sugar, butter, egg, and vanilla until well combined. Fold in the dry ingredients and mix thoroughly. Stir in the chocolate chips and transfer the mixture to the prepared pan.

4 Bake for 30 to 35 minutes, until the top is lightly browned and cracked. Let cool completely, then carefully lift out of the pan using the parchment paper. Cut into squares.

> **RECIPE RIFF**
>
> **Skillet Blondie Sundaes:** Bake the batter in a greased cast-iron pan instead of a square pan. Serve warm with vanilla ice cream and chocolate sauce.

Classic Hummus, page 56

measurement conversions

VOLUME EQUIVALENTS (LIQUID)

US STANDARD	US STANDARD (OUNCES)	METRIC (APPROX.)
2 tablespoons	1 fl. oz.	30 mL
¼ cup	2 fl. oz.	60 mL
½ cup	4 fl. oz.	120 mL
1 cup	8 fl. oz.	240 mL
1½ cups	12 fl. oz.	355 mL
2 cups or 1 pint	16 fl. oz.	475 mL
4 cups or 1 quart	32 fl. oz.	1 L
1 gallon	128 fl. oz.	4 L

OVEN TEMPERATURES

FAHRENHEIT (F)	CELSIUS (C) (APPROX.)
250°	120°
300°	150°
325°	165°
350°	180°
375°	190°
400°	200°
425°	220°
450°	230°

VOLUME EQUIVALENTS (DRY)

US STANDARD	METRIC (APPROX.)
⅛ teaspoon	0.5 mL
¼ teaspoon	1 mL
½ teaspoon	2 mL
¾ teaspoon	4 mL
1 teaspoon	5 mL
1 tablespoon	15 mL
¼ cup	59 mL
⅓ cup	79 mL
½ cup	118 mL
⅔ cup	156 mL
¾ cup	177 mL
1 cup	235 mL
2 cups or 1 pint	475 mL
3 cups	700 mL
4 cups or 1 quart	1 L

WEIGHT EQUIVALENTS

US STANDARD	METRIC (APPROX.)
½ ounce	15 g
1 ounce	30 g
2 ounces	60 g
4 ounces	115 g
8 ounces	225 g
12 ounces	340 g
16 ounces or 1 pound	455 g

index

acknowledgments

A huge debt of gratitude goes to my husband, Adam. He has been my number one cheerleader for the last 20 years. He helped taste test most of the recipes in this book, and if you know Adam, he always gives an honest opinion! I am eternally grateful to have him as my partner and best friend and couldn't have done this without his emotional support. Thank you so much.

I also want to thank my children, Keira and Connor, who were always willing to taste recipes (especially the cookies). I am so proud of both of you, and I hope you always feel that my success is yours as well. It is my hope that you will find your passion in life like I found mine. I will support both of you always!

To my grandmother Opal, who instilled a love of cooking in me from a young age. You and Gramps taught me what love looks like, and I don't know how I could have grown up without you. I have many fond memories in your blue kitchen, rolling sugar cookies, making root beer floats, and of course washing dishes in your big porcelain sink. Love you always.

I would be remiss if I didn't thank the many friends I have made through my YouTube journey. Thank you to Christine, who was always there for me to vent to and bounce ideas off! Thank you to my sister Kristen, for helping me with recipe ideas and encouraging me. And to all my viewers and subscribers, my utmost gratitude, because without you, this would not have been possible!

about the author

JEN CHAPIN grew up in rural Iowa and has over 20 years of home cooking experience. In 2018, Jen began a YouTube channel centered around food and lifestyle content, with the goal of supporting home cooks and working moms. Her channel has now grown to over 100,000 subscribers, and she has published hundreds of cooking videos.

Jen lives in Eastern Iowa with her husband, Adam, her daughter, Keira, and her son, Connor. She holds a master's degree in nursing administration and works as a health-care analyst by day. On evenings and weekends, you'll find her in the kitchen cooking or working on her YouTube channel, Jen Chapin.

Connect with Jen on Instagram @JenChapin, on YouTube at Jen Chapin Videos, or on her website, Jen-Chapin.com.

CPSIA information can be obtained
at www.ICGtesting.com
Printed in the USA
LVHW010104260421
685329LV00002B/4